O R
MIRACLES

"With humor and spunk, Rachel Gerber takes us on a wondrous, demanding Emmaus journey all her own, where she recognizes God and returns to spread the word. Good news for other parents needing encouragement in their own parenting!"
—Bonnie Miller-McLemore, author of *In the Midst of Chaos: Care of Children as Spiritual Practice*

"This book will put a shine into any beleaguered day. With sparkling transparency, Rachel reveals the mess and marvel of life with little people. Amid a cascade of daily chaos, she breaks open ordinary moments with such winsome vulnerability that I was captivated anew by the holy wonder of it all."
—Sara Wenger Shenk, president of Anabaptist Mennonite Biblical Seminary

"As a grandmother, I continually remembered young parents I know and love while reading this book. Rachel creates vivid images in which other young parents can find themselves, but then digs deeper to unearth and share her early parenthood spiritual journey. As she uncovers the holy in the midst of growing laundry piles and disrupted nights, she offers lifelines of hope and inspiration to other overwhelmed bearers of God's blessings."
—Elsie Rempel, author of *Please Pass the Faith: The Art of Spiritual Grandparenting*

"This book is warm, wise, funny, and full of real-life moments with the author and her family. Rachel's storytelling and spiritual insight are great gifts that I look forward to sharing with others, especially with parents of young children. An inspiring and thoughtful book."

—April Yamasaki, author of *Sacred Pauses: Spiritual Practices for Personal Renewal*

"In her own straightforward, energetic voice, Rachel Gerber invites you into her world; a world brimming with boisterous boys, plenty of work, and a whiff of the Holy. As she recounts parenting peaks and valleys, she invites us to see God calling and caring for us, even—or especially—in seemingly mundane moments."

—Hannah Heinzekehr, director of communications and marketing, Mennonite Church USA

ORDINARY
MIRACLES

AWAKENING *to*
the HOLY WORK
of PARENTING

RACHEL S. GERBER

Much joy
fa the journey!
Rachel

Herald Press
Harrisonburg, Virginia
Kitchener, Ontario

Library of Congress Cataloging-in-Publication Data
Gerber, Rachel S., 1978-
  Ordinary miracles : awakening to the holy work of parent-
ing / Rachel S. Gerber.
    pages cm
  ISBN 978-0-8361-9857-7 (pbk. : alk. paper) 1. Spirituality-
-Christianity. 2. God (Christianity)--Worship and love. 3.
Bible. Luke, XXIV, 13-35--Criticism, interpretation, etc. 4.
Parenting--Religious aspects--Christianity. I. Title.
  BV4501.3.G467 2014
  248.8'45--dc23
                                          2013040593

ORDINARY MIRACLES
Copyright © 2014 by Herald Press, Harrisonburg, Virginia
22802
  Released simultaneously in Canada by Herald Press,
  Kitchener, Ontario N2G 3R1. All rights reserved.
Library of Congress Control Number: 2013040593
International Standard Book Number: 978-0-8361-9857-7
Printed in United States of America
Cover design by Reuben Graham, design by Reuben Graham
Cover photo by mrcdoublet / iStock / Thinkstock

Unless otherwise indicated, all Scripture quotations are tak-
en from the Holy Bible, New Living Translation, copyright
© 1996, 2004, 2007 by Tyndale House Foundation. Used by
permission of Tyndale House Publishers, Inc., Carol Stream,
Illinois 60188. All rights reserved.

Scripture marked (*The Message*) taken from *The Message*.
Copyright © 1993, 1994, 1995, 1996, 2000, 2001, 2002.
Used by permission of NavPress Publishing Group.

To order or request information, please call 1-800-245-
7894 in the U.S. or 1-800-631-6535 in Canada. Or visit
www.heraldpress.com.

18 17 16 15 14   10 9 8 7 6 5 4 3 2 1

For Shawn, my companion all along the way. What a joy it is to journey with you.

And to my boys, Owen, Connor, and Zachary. Through you I have seen God.

The best things are the nearest: breath in your nostrils, light in your eyes, flowers at your feet, duties at your hand, the path of God just before you. Then do not grasp at the stars, but do life's plain, common work as it comes, certain that daily duties and daily bread are the sweetest things in life.

—widely attributed to Robert Louis Stevenson

CONTENTS

FOREWORD

Having little children is tough. If you are in this season, you know the truth of my words. If you have moved out of this season, you know it even better.

When we are in the middle of a difficult time, we can't always appreciate what exactly we are wandering through. Some days we feel on top of the world, and some days we can't figure out why we are exhausted and emotional and feeling lost and overwhelmed.

When I was in my most challenging motherhood season—the one in which I had four boys under the age of five—I would explain to my doctor that I was feeling "a little tired." I could never figure out why that made her laugh. When my boys were little, I could never comprehend the joy that independent bathroom visits would one day bring—for me or for them! Children do grow up and learn to sleep through the night and feed themselves and walk safely from a store to a car. Oh, the joy of self-sufficiency!

Motherhood in all its seasons has its own unique challenges. But truly, that sweet time of caring for small children offers what few other mothering seasons can: twenty-four-hour, never-let-up, carrying, feeding, watching-like-a-hawk exhaustion. You live for naptime, and bedtime is a kiss from Jesus. These years are delightful. They don't last forever, which is bittersweet.

And in the midst of it all, God is there.

We laugh about the challenges because it keeps us sane, and we seek solace and wisdom in the difficult times. And there God is, walking beside us.

What a blessing and a joy when we discover this truth. What a relief and consolation when we recognize that God is with us every step of the way. In the sleepless nights, in the lonely hours, in those moments when I think life is passing me by as the rest of the free world moves ahead: God is right here, sitting beside me.

God gives us himself, and he gives the gift of others, too. He sends us encouragement and joy, and we walk with others along the way. We are built up and loved and reminded that we can do it. We are doing what God has asked us to do, and he sends his grace and peace to get the job done. Today, you are called to wipe a toddler's nose. You are being Jesus to the person in front of you.

As Rachel Gerber so beautifully reminds us here, God walks beside us. We don't always see him, but he is there. We are not alone in this journey—we have brothers and sisters who walk beside us, too. Even at our most lonely and discouraged, God has given us everything we need.

This book is a beautiful reminder that we are on a journey and that it can be a challenge but that God is with us as we make our way. Like the disciples, we don't always recognize God's presence, but like the disciples, we are not alone.

This book reminds us to seek—and we shall indeed find.

—Rachel Balducci
author of *How Do You Tuck In a Superhero?*,
blogger at www.testosterhome.net,
mother of six

PROLOGUE

Beyond the How-To Manuals

I've done a lot of jobs in my life. I've had traditional ones as an elementary school teacher, a minister, and a writer. And I've had my fair share of the unconventional: library custodian, commercial voice-over artist, and basket-weaving instructor. But I can honestly say that nothing has given me greater insight into the crazy depth of the love of God than being a parent.

By far, being a mother has been the most difficult and most rewarding role I have ever had. My vocation as a mother has stretched me, shaped me, and sometimes even squashed me much more than any of these other jobs. Period.

Before I get too far, I need to mention that I believe it makes not a lick of difference how a child in your life comes into being. Whether it is through your own birthing, through foster care or adoption, through being an uncle or aunt, or through being a neighbor of a child you love and cherish—no matter how these little people come into life—caring for them can often feel so challenging. They demand so much. They suck out time, sleep, energy, and the ability to feel even somewhat effective and efficient.

But let me make this crystal clear: with my whole heart, even through all this, I love my children. I love them to the depths of the ocean and to the heights of the universe and back. Over and over again. And maybe just a *teensy* bit more when they are sleeping. This miraculous love I have discovered, even in the trenches of parenting, has awakened in me a new inner sight. For I finally understand. The love I have for my spunky and beautiful boys is a mirror reflection of the love that God has *for me*. In many ways, my children have awakened in me this awareness, for they have enabled me to see the very face of God. They have awakened my inner eye to understand the depth of love that is far greater than I had previously known. It has opened my eyes to encounter love, to offer love, to *be* love. I understand this in an inside-out way. So in many ways, the God I encounter day in and day out through my children is the God who is saving me. My children enable me to understand who God is, how God comes, and where God journeys with me.

This book is not a parenting how-to manual, although I tell stories from my own parenting experience. It is not full of tips and tricks on how to make thirty meals with one pound of ground beef (because, *obviously*, this is the best way of embracing your Proverbs 31 woman mojo). It is not about how to wake up earlier to read your Bible for personal quiet time. Because, if you are like me, you've already been awake four times during the night because someone needed to nurse and someone else wet the bed. To suggest that connecting with God can only be done by finding silent moments for quiet reflection before your family wakes up is simply absurd. Life in this stage rarely allows for silence, and to rise before anyone else means a certain future of never sleeping again.

This book is also absolutely not a book to pit at-home parents against employed parents, because God-honoring work lies in many spheres and because there is more than enough grace for all. Rather, this book is about my own frail awakening to how the love I offer, the time I invest, the attention I give to my crazy, syrupy-sweet little boys is really about loving and serving the God who created them. Being their mama is just as much a ministry for me now as the ministry I had when I worked as a pastor in a church setting. But this is a ministry of the hearth, and my congregation now consists of very short people.

In this book, I want to share with you about how God surprises me all along the way as I care for my own brood, providing just enough bread for the journey to see me through each day. Most of the time I fail to see the holy moments because I am blinded by the monotony of the daily routine or exasperated by the unexpected messes that only little ones can create.

In short, this book is not so much about my children as it is about me, their mama. It is about how, through them, I am catching glimpses of not only who God is but also who God is calling me to be. I hope that you will find yourself in the midst of my story and discover God's invitation to you.

Let's be real: for parents of small children, life is full. We don't need even one more thing to do. I'm already so honored that you are taking your precious limited time to read this book rather than take a nap. There are already many obstacles that we as young parents face in finding time to connect with God. Yet despite the fact that it is hard to carve out the time to pray, I desperately need it. I crave this time, because this connection with Love is what enables me to love deeper. So what is there to do?

Maybe our spiritual quest isn't so much about us finding God as it is about awakening to the Presence that always comes. What if it is really more about God finding *us*? How are we being invited to take notice of where God already *is*? Could connection with God come even as we change diapers, fold laundry, help with homework, and haul kids to soccer practice, music lessons, and story hour?

A meaningful allegory about this longing and awakening is the biblical story found in Luke 24. Often called the "Road to Emmaus," this is the story in which Jesus secretly accompanies two utterly weary followers as they walk along. When they welcome him into their home and share bread with one another, their eyes are opened, and they see that this stranger is really not a stranger at all, but the One they were searching for all along the way. And then, just as quickly as they recognize him, he disappears.

In many ways, the Emmaus story has been a guiding story to my own life. As a parent, I live the story of this road every day. Often, I live it multiple times. It's the cycle between sheer exasperation and utter elation. It is exhausting. It is disorienting. It is often just plain crazy. Sometimes I cry, sometimes I yell, and sometimes I just have to go ahead and laugh because of the hilarity of life with boys. Yet the rewarding part for me comes as I find myself surprised by the Divine in the midst of it all and learning to find joy in the managed chaos of life. (With boys, *managed* is the operative word!)

Ultimately, this collection is part of a greater Story about hope. It shows how Love is present in our darkest hour of greatest disorientation, in our most mundane days, and in moments of exhilaration of joy and beauty when we finally awaken to the blessings of life. God surprises. We awaken and see ordinary miracles all around.

One more thing before we begin: the stories that follow are organized according to the chronological timeline of the Emmaus Road rather than the order of my own life events. I tell the events of the Emmaus Road story in the order in which they occurred and then hook my life experiences and reflections to the biblical story, rather than the other way around. This approach enables me to tell my own story of awakening to the presence of God that always comes in *kairos* time, which is God's time, rather than *chronos* time, which is ours. Like the story of the disciples on the way to Emmaus, my story ping-pongs from bewilderment to joy to sadness and back to joy again. It includes the ordinary texture of days with small children and experiences of tragedy and grief that made me question everything I thought I knew about God. Ultimately, my story is one of slowly awakening to the Christ who comes to us beyond the boundaries of time and circumstance.

So will you join me in daring to open your eyes and truly see the One who has always been, is, and will continue to be? The disciples did not travel alone toward Emmaus; they did it in the company of each other. I invite you to awaken to how Christ meets us all along the way so that we might return with burning hearts and declare together, "I have seen the Lord!"

Peace,

—Rachel
www.everything-belongs.com

THE ROAD
TO EMMAUS

Luke 24:13-35

That same day two of Jesus' followers were walking to the village of Emmaus, seven miles from Jerusalem. As they walked along they were talking about everything that had happened. As they talked and discussed these things, Jesus himself suddenly came and began walking with them. But God kept them from recognizing him.

He asked them, "What are you discussing so intently as you walk along?"

They stopped short, sadness written across their faces. Then one of them, Cleopas, replied, "You must be the only person in Jerusalem who hasn't heard about all the things that have happened there the last few days."

"What things?" Jesus asked.

"The things that happened to Jesus, the man from Nazareth," they said. "He was a prophet who did powerful miracles, and he was a mighty teacher in the eyes of God and all the people. But our leading priests and other religious leaders handed him over to be condemned to death, and they crucified him. We had hoped he was the Messiah who had come to rescue Israel. This all happened three days ago.

"Then some women from our group of his followers were at his tomb early this morning, and they came back with an amazing report. They said his body was missing, and they had seen angels who told them Jesus is alive! Some of our men ran out to see, and sure enough, his body was gone, just as the women had said."

Then Jesus said to them, "You foolish people! You find it so hard to believe all that the prophets wrote in the Scriptures. Wasn't it clearly predicted that the Messiah would have to suffer all these things before entering his glory?" Then Jesus took them through the writings of Moses and all the prophets, explaining from all the Scriptures the things concerning himself.

By this time they were nearing Emmaus and the end of their journey. Jesus acted as if he were going on, but they begged him, "Stay the night with us, since it is getting late." So he went home with them. As they sat down to eat, he took the bread and blessed it. Then he broke it and gave it to them. Suddenly, their eyes were opened, and they recognized him. And at that moment he disappeared!

They said to each other, "Didn't our hearts burn within us as he talked with us on the road and explained the Scriptures to us?" And within the hour they were on their way back to Jerusalem. There they found the eleven disciples and the others who had gathered with them, who said, "The Lord has really risen! He appeared to Peter."

Then the two from Emmaus told their story of how Jesus had appeared to them as they were walking along the road, and how they had recognized him as he was breaking the bread.

Chapter 1

I DON'T KNOW ANYTHING

······································

"But they were not able
to recognize who he was."
—Luke 24:16 (*The Message*)

······································

I actually killed a cactus once. I mean, really: who kills a *cactus*? So when I discovered that I was pregnant with my first child, my first thought was, *What have I done?* Could I really handle growing a human being? God knows my record with gardening.

I kept having a recurring dream about forgetting my soon-to-be baby. The locations would change—grocery store, car, house—but the premise was always the same. Was the combination of plant and dream a prophesy waiting to come true? I felt doomed.

I don't think you can ever prepare yourself for having a child. Baby showers try, with the cutesy games in which well-wishers give their best, most trusted advice on the care of all things infant. How to swaddle, which car seat is the safest, and where to point the little penis so as to not get sprayed in the face.

But there is nothing anyone can say, nothing you can read, nothing you can *do* to actually prepare for the combination of awe and wonder, elation and joy, and panic and despair when you are handed a child of your own.

I. Don't. Know. Anything.

This was my exact thought as the doctors handed me my slippery and screaming babe, whom we named Owen, at 6:08 p.m. on August 29, 2006. As I gazed into the most gorgeous, scrunched face, my heart was amazed at the miracle in front of me. And I was completely shell-shocked.

Within the hour, as the fluorescent lights blinked overhead, the nurse wheeled me from the faux wood delivery room to the mint-green postpartum room. There I recovered from the forceps delivery, made only slightly less traumatic through the miraculous invention of an epidural. Trying to remember to breathe, with an almost numbing awe, I continued to gape at this marvel beside me.

It was in this warm postpartum nest, with the lights turned low, that the nurse parked my little eight-pound, seven-ounce, forty-one-week-old peanut. (Yes, this little one needed to be evicted.) She had swaddled him tightly and placed him in the bassinet next to me. She laid her hand on my shoulder and looked at my husband, Shawn, and then at me.

"Congratulations again," she said. "What a cute little guy. The bassinet holds the diapers and wipes. And there are extra onesies underneath."

Then she turned around and walked out, closing the door behind her.

In a panic, I shot my eyes up to Shawn. *Wa-wait! She just left us. Oh my goodness, she just left us!*

I wasn't anticipating doing this quite yet. It hadn't even been an hour since this little one had been veiled and hidden from me. Now I was the one in charge of diapers and changing and feeding? *Note to self: write this on my advice card at the next baby shower.*

Although this pregnancy was long desired, planned for, and highly expected, in that moment I realized that in saying yes to this wonderful new adventure in life, I was also opening myself wide to so many unknowns.

Ready or not, here it comes.

There is nothing restful about being in a hospital. Nurses come in, hour after hour, to poke and prod. Doctors make rounds at ungodly hours, followed by the residents, and then the interns, who ask the same questions over and over again. *Remind me: Why did we choose to deliver our baby in a teaching hospital?* No, the only restful thing about being in a hospital is when said interns, checked by the residents, double-checked by the doctors, say we can finally go home.

Once we received our clearance to leave on that third day, I dressed Owen in his adorable hand-smocked, fine brown-and-blue plaid outfit to go home. It took much longer to clothe him than I ever expected. The cuteness factor of the darling romper quickly diminished: twenty minutes later I was still attempting to navigate the world's smallest buttons on newborn legs that were coiled like a spring. Oh how I wished that

I had thrown the one-piece zipper pajamas in the diaper bag. Whoever insisted on putting microscopic buttons on newborn clothing should pretty much lose their job, because they obviously don't have children of their own and don't know a thing about dressing real-life babies.

As I settled Owen down into his car seat, weaving and buckling straps, the chasm between us now seemed too great. How does a heart learn to fiercely love a stranger so quickly? Because, really, that was what he still was to us: a stranger. Although we had been so close for nine months, the sinews of flesh had hidden us from one another. I had felt him move, and he had enjoyed what I ate, and we had played games of poke and wiggle. But I could only imagine what this little person looked like, how his personality would emerge, and who he would become.

There were just so many questions, and only time would begin to uncover the answers of the deep.

I quickly learned that there is nothing restful about coming home from the hospital, either.

Eyes full of tears, I looked up to my own mother, who had flown in from Pennsylvania and who now had a new name: *Grandma*. I asked her if it was possible to die of exhaustion. I felt fairly certain that I was on my last leg. I considered asking my husband, a chaplain, to kneel at my side and perform last rites.

How can someone so small change your life in such gigantic ways?

I never thought parenting would be easy. But I never could have imagined the wholly demanding and self-sacrificial nature of it all. Nothing about my body was mine anymore. Nothing about my time was mine. My days and my nights were his. It was all so disorienting. Of course, I was more than happy to give these things. I would have gladly given my own life for this little package, who was still in so many ways such a mystery to me.

I wasn't asking for much. I know that three-day-old babies are not able to give a whole lot. Except for poop. This he gave freely.

I wasn't asking for a verbal thank you for sustaining his life. I wasn't even asking for a smile.

How about just a little eye contact?

Before too long, instead of an infant swaddled, he was off running and playing, climbing, and talking a blue streak. Just as children begin to gain some independence, you think you can do it again. Oh, how memories fade. I am pretty sure this is a God-given strategy to keep the human race from the danger of extinction.

Two days less than twenty-seven months later—on Thanksgiving Day—we welcomed our second son, Connor. I remember being absolutely elated and could think of no better holiday on which to give birth. Truly it was a day to give thanks.

Soon, however, I found myself back again in the swarm of sleepless nights, except now they were coupled with a busy two-year-old. *Come, Lord Jesus, come.* Both were so precious and yet so demanding. My eyes were blinded by the multiple tasks of life. Like the disciples on the road to Emmaus, I didn't recognize the One who joins me on the journey.

I often found myself going through the motions, getting wrapped up in the daily chores of life. Meal preparation, laundry, nail-trimming. (With little boys, keeping up with hygiene could almost be a part-time job.) I saw my kids and all they needed; I saw the schedule and all it contained; I saw the laundry and how it continued to grow; and I felt the burden of picking up my feet to do it all again, and again, and again. Today, tomorrow, and the day after that.

Life, especially with small children, can so easily overwhelm. Frankly, it caused me to second-guess any and all of my motives for reproducing in the first place. I started to wonder what life would be like if I were still working as a teacher or a minister, which I had done before. I wondered what life would be like if I were a news anchor on the *Today Show*, which was my newest fantasy. Oh, the joy and stimulation I would feel at shutting the door and walking outside. Oh, to leave behind the chaos and the whining and the arguing and the rambunctious play that usually ends in tears. Because, over time, it just builds up, and up, and up.

I don't think anyone really wants to be around when it finally explodes.

But this is not how it is supposed to be, I kept thinking. *Where is the joy? Where is the peace?*

Where is the patience? Because I'm pretty sure that Monster Parent is not on the list of fruits of the Spirit.

One question haunted me: *What am I doing?*

I am not talking about the more superficial version of that question: of walking into the same room a gazillion times with no more clue as to what you are looking for than you did the last time. That's what I call "baby brain." It is quite amazing how babies can just suck the grey matter out.

What I mean is the deep, raw, keeping-you-up-at-night form of the question: *What am I doing?* Parenting was making me feel as though my head were being twisted and turned in a million directions, and all of the competencies that I had—or thought I had—were shattered. Talk about a reality check.

What am I doing? How in the world do I ever think I can raise a human being? Sometimes, when I was honest—really, really honest—I answered my own question.

I . . . don't . . . know.

What I had *thought* parenting should look like, feel like, and be like wasn't at all the same as the reality of what parenting *was* like. That is an awfully hard intersection at which to live.

Where are you, God, in this craze? I kept thinking. *Everything just seems so mixed up.*

When children come along, loyalties to vocation are often stretched and pulled in ways one could previously not imagine. I had been an elementary education major during college and had never dreamed of becoming a pastor. Yet my call to the ministry ended up leading me to pastorates at large Mennonite churches, first in Indiana and then in Colorado. What an honor and privilege it was to serve the people of God in this way.

Being a slight anomaly—a young, female Mennonite pastor in the West—I was given plenty of opportunities to do wider work in the denomination. I was asked to lead worship for our binational convention, where over six thousand youth and adults gathered for a week. I had a monthly column in a national churchwide magazine, and I was soon coauthoring two books of skits and activities for kids and congregations. Life was full, and it was invigorating being at the intersection where need and call meet.

But part-time work is never truly part time when one works with people, especially in the ministry. You can't love people and use a punch card. It simply doesn't work. In time, pastoral ministry felt too much for me, and my ministerial stole began to feel more like an albatross around my neck than a vestment of grace and call. I knew it was time to say goodbye to my church family in order to more fully embrace my own. Soon after I was ordained and we moved to a new city, I left pastoral work to become a full-time parent.

In those early days after choosing to leave my professional vocation of ministry to embark on at-home parenthood, I often felt like I was standing on shifting sand. Questions plagued me. *Who am I? What are my gifts? How am I offering them to others?*

One January, I attended an annual leadership training conference that was held at the seminary I attended in Harrisonburg, Virginia. It was so wonderful to be back in academia, attending seminars that rebooted my brain and engaged me in higher-level thinking. The highest level of thinking I usually attained at home occurred when someone pushed the wrong button on the TV remote and I had to figure out why all the lights were blinking red.

Yes, I was grateful to find that I could still think. It was also fabulous to reconnect with some of the others from my cohort during seminary days. Conversing with them, I heard about the amazing ways that they were working and making a difference in the world around them. They were equipping and training leaders in Africa, pursuing doctoral studies, and growing their churches. Plus, they all seemed really happy. And really fulfilled. Could I say the same?

If I was honest, my life often felt like desert wandering. I felt the heat of the sun that somehow raged from within. I was full of envy of those who seemed to be doing more, offering their gifts to the church in more concrete, professional ways. I felt the cold of the desert night, wondering if the light of my own gifts was dimming. Would anything be left of my brain and my gifts when this season of life was over, or would Barney have completely washed them all away?

Over and over I told myself, *I am shaping lives. I am doing a wonderful thing. This choice to be at home is something I will never regret. Right? Right?* But trying to figure out exactly who I was now, balancing my own call to the ministry and my life as a mom, left me feeling more than a bit perplexed. Just how was I using my gifts? Did my ordination make a mockery of my life now, filled as it was with diapers? Had I really been called to ministry, or had I simply misinterpreted the signs?

But mostly it was the routine and monotony that got to me. Sometimes it was the unexpected things that each day brought that nearly put me over the edge. It was the cheetah spots that the boys drew all over their bodies with permanent marker. It was the bowls full of milk on the kitchen floor (and milk *on* the kitchen floor) while they pretended to be pet cats. It was the bottle of nail polish they had decided to use to paint each other's nails. In the car. Times like these added just enough crazy to the day to make this mama laugh and cry all at the same time.

EMMAUS ROAD
··

Nothing made sense anymore for the two
disciples who took that long road out of
Jerusalem toward Emmaus, either. They both
felt exhausted and disoriented, overwhelmed and
abandoned—but only one was named.

Cleopas.

Luke 24 offers no notion about the other, but
it could have been any name, like Roger, Heidi,
Jen, Mandy, Chet, or maybe, just maybe, Rachel.

Because I know.

I know the feeling of disillusionment and sleep
deprivation when everything seems upside down
and exhaustion clouds purpose. Like the disciples,
I often wonder where God is. In the midst of this
stretching and taxing season of caring for little
people, how would I even be able to find the time
to seek God out? I could barely even find the time
and space to take a shower.

In the midst of the disorientation and bewilderment, the disciples could not see the One who
approached them. Like me, *They. Knew. Nothing.
Either.*

Chapter 2

COMPANION ON THE JOURNEY

....

"Jesus himself suddenly came
and began walking with them."
—Luke 24:15

....

Although the days with small children seemed to wear on endlessly, the nights seemed longer. Always. I often found myself feeling anxious come the four o'clock hour in the afternoon, because I knew that evening would soon appear. And then would come the night, with all its unknowns. Would I sleep? Would I *ever* sleep again?

I remember one particularly difficult night when Owen just screamed and screamed. And, if it was possible, screamed some more. Nothing would pacify this babe. How could something so small bellow so loud? Shawn and I tried everything. We adjusted the swaddle. We rocked. We bounced. We walked outside. We walked inside. We jiggled to the right. We jiggled to the left. Nothing worked. He just wanted to scream and cry and make sure I knew just how unhappy he was about life at the given moment. There was nothing I could do.

Colic is an evil, evil thing.

But it was then—somewhere between the step, the jiggle, the half-shake left, the step-over shake, and the shake right—that it struck me.

I am exactly like Owen.

I scream, I cry, I complain, and I writhe about my life. I am often unsettled in body, mind, and soul. I grasp for more, search for more, and claw for something to pacify me in my long night. I wonder where God is. I wonder how I am using my gifts. I worry that any future vocational opportunities will be null and void when I finally emerge from this season of tending the hearth—a season that I actually was privileged to choose.

Here I stand, spewing resentment and anguish, convinced that I have been left all alone.

Quietly, I sit in the hallway, under the cloak of darkness. Waiting. Watching. Ready to pounce. Will my toddler get out of bed?

Again?

Here I sit at the end of the day, literally at the end of my rope. For the love of God, will the child *please* go to sleep?

In the dark, in the corner, I find tears streaming down my cheeks. *Why can't I do better? Be better? My tongue is short, my nerves are shot, my patience is fried. All day.*

I won the Monster Mother Award today. And yesterday. And perhaps even the day before that, too.

What is happening?

As I sit, burying my palms into the stinging wetness, I wonder what I am teaching my children. How to yell well? How to lose your temper?

"Mommy angry?" the little one constantly asks me. "Mommy angry? Mommy happy?"

Is this the legacy I will leave? God, I hope not.

The tears of honest reflection sting.

A good tree produces good fruit. And the fruits of the Spirit are love, joy, peace, patience, kindness, faithfulness, gentleness, and self-control. A good tree cannot produce bad fruit, and a bad tree cannot produce good fruit.

What am I producing?

I can chalk it up to being tired, feeling sick, and wondering if I did the right thing by quitting my job. I can chalk it up to the challenging stages of my children, or to the recent interruptions to their schedule, or even to the barometric pressure.

But the litmus test at the end of the day asks for fruit.

I haven't been showing well. I'd say I'm rather diseased and buggy; I have blight.

Who wants that?

"Mom, do you want to play with me?"

This is a question that I hear no less than one gazillion times a day. Give or take a few.

Right now? This very instant? It's eight o'clock in the morning. My coffee is still hot and I've got emails to check. Lists to make. Laundry to fold. Dishes to do. Play? Now?

"Play with me, please?"

Blink. Blink.

It gets me every time. How can I refuse his sweet face?

I rise, leaving the table and those details that will always be there to play with the little one who will not.

He says to me, "You hide. I'll seek. One, two, three . . ." I race to find a decent hiding place before my speed-counting munchkin reaches ten. Quietly, I pull back the shower curtain and step in without a sound.

And wait.

In the darkness, I hide.

"Mom? *Mom?* Where are you?"

As I stand there, fully clothed behind that shower curtain, I realize that this is not just a game of child's play. It is much more than that. For I know who is really calling out to me, wondering where I am: the One who is seeking me, always searching, always longing—the same as he did in the garden of Eden so long before.

And here I am hiding. In the dark.

I think about how often I find myself like this. I am ashamed of how often I fail on this journey of faith; lacking patience and compassion, I am instead full of self-centeredness, jealousy, and resentment. The list could go on.

I cower. And hide. What good am I? How could God want me?

Use me?

And yet, out of God's extravagant love and compassion, God comes. Seeking until he finds.

This love is not about what I do or don't do. Just as I can't earn God's love, I can't stop it, either.

The lights flick on. Little fingers wrap themselves around the curtain and pull it open. Brown eyes as big as the moon itself light up with sheer delight. Pure joy abounds.

"Found you!" he screeches as he reaches in for a bear hug. Arms wrapped tight in love. Yes and yes.

Love finds. Love always finds.

But the question lingers: *Do I really want to be found?*

❧

One morning as I plodded around the track next to our home, training for a ten-kilometer race, I realized how I was running. I'm not talking about "heel, toe, heel, toe" or about keeping my arms poised at perfect ninety-degree angles.

It was my eyes.

They were glued to the ground about a foot in front of me. A voice from within said, "Look around."

And so I did. As I lifted my head, my sight was filled with a beautiful sunrise and lush green trees. It was a beautiful morning. Huffing my way around the track, I realized how often I go through my day with my eyes downward, focused only within my little world and on how the hot sand stings. How easy it is for me to get caught up in the demands of life and to feel overwhelmed, torn, fragmented. As any parent of small children can, I easily lose perspective on the bigger picture.

I see the piles of laundry and dishes to be done, the toys to be picked up, and the errands to run.

How long have I forgotten? Life is not only about drudgery, chores, tasks, and work. I am blessed, I realized, because I actually have people to love and care for. As long as there are people in my life to care for, laundry will be. Dishes will be. Messes will be. Errands will be.

I breathed in, exhaled, and was dumbfounded at this grace that filled my life.

The ironic part of it all? When I got back home that morning, sweaty but energized, Shawn told me that during my run, he and the boys had stood on our front steps for a bit and watched me run.

They had been waving and cheering me on.

I had had no clue.

Which makes me wonder: *What else have I been missing?*

Learning to lift my eyes, to unglue them from the ground, did not suddenly come easily to me after I learned it on that run. If such things were easy, I wouldn't have had to write a whole book about them.

Living in this state of expectation—a posture in which we anticipate encountering ordinary miracles throughout each day—takes work. It takes effort to remember. It is just so easy to forget the sacred mundane through which we walk every day.

&

The clock reads 7:30 a.m. My son toddles forward, holding a book. *A book? Right now?*

My coffee sits here hot. And I would really like to drink it while it is still hot. A book would make it lukewarm at best. And, by the way, it's only 7:30 *in the morning.* The hour for stillness to prepare and plan for and pray about the day ahead, with my *hot* coffee. *Sesame Street* plays in the background but does not tempt him today.

I wonder if Mary ever forgot the holy she had birthed? I wonder if, when Jesus was a toddler, Mary ever wanted to drink her coffee hot?

"Lap. Up on lap," my son coaxes. He crawls up with book in hand. As I reluctantly make space, pushing the dark morning drug away, he snuggles in close. The warmth of fleece sheets radiates from his skin. The smell of sweetness lingers.

I breathe in. The Spirit fills me.

Looking into my eyes, he smiles. His big toothy grin comes close and kisses me. Through the fog of the months of interrupted sleep and building resentment about having to drink microwaved coffee, I am surprised by the joy that grows as I make space on my lap. Maybe this is what I really need. Maybe opening my arms wider to embrace the reality of what my life is full of now, rather than crossing my arms tighter and refusing to give any more, is how to get through these crazy days and find fulfillment.

Could this be how love comes? With frazzled hair, I snuggle Connor close for half-a-nanosecond before he wiggles free to lumber off toward Elmo's world. Is it true, I wonder, that God could be so close to me—running around me, jumping on me, karate-kicking in front of me—that I completely miss it? Could it be that in my own blindness I am actually pushing God away rather than embracing the One who continually comes?

I laugh at how I think that my cup of ~~hot~~ . . . ~~warm~~ . . . *tepid* coffee is what I need to awaken each day. Maybe what I *really* need is to make space for the little ones who long to be with me. To open myself fully and embrace the Gift that comes, receiving the silent whisper of what my own soul longs to hear:

This: *You are loved just as you are, wherever you are, because you are enough.*

And this: *You have people to love.*

EMMAUS ROAD
. . . .

The disciples on the road to Emmaus simply could not connect the dots. It all seemed so confusing and disorienting. They had heard with their own ears that the tomb was empty, but there was no body.

Jesus was *still* gone.

What good are stories, if there is no one to run to?

But despite their heartache and confusion at the loss of their teacher, the disciples were intrigued by the stranger who joined them along the way. The identity of the stranger was hidden from them, and they could not see the Gift that met them as they wallowed in their own preoccupations. Even though they still did not recognize him, Christ was present, never leaving their side.

Who are the Christs I meet every day? Like the disciples, I find that Christ is always surprising me, challenging me, guiding me, and inviting me to change my perspective from simply walking the ordinary to living the sacred mundane.

As they approached the town that evening, perhaps the sky was turning orange and purple. As the last rays of light were quickly swallowed by the horizon and their own shadows lengthened with each step, the disciples stopped and turned to the one who had accompanied them the journey long. They paused to invite this stranger, now turned companion and friend, to temporarily cease his own journey and come home with them for the night.

Little did they know that the One they had been longing for had been with them the whole way.

And now, as they crossed the threshold, there he stood. *Right in the middle of their very own home.*

Chapter 3

SLOWING DOWN, COMING HOME

. . . .

"[T]hey begged him, 'Stay the night
with us, since it is getting late.'
So he went home with them."
—Luke 24:29

. . . .

I recently packed for a fourteen-hour drive and five-day holiday. The boys, sensing the excitement and novelty of what was coming, were literally bouncing off the walls. They do not understand that if the house is in some semblance of order before we leave for vacation, unpacking is so much easier when we return home. *Please don't throw, dump, unpack, spill, or crunch* becomes my mantra at such times. And wrestling, which usually ends with someone in tears, doesn't add well to this mix either.

Throw in a husband who is doing another twenty-four-hour shift on call at work, and things can feel pretty distressing.

Deep breath. Deep breath. Chronos time ticks.

Chronos is the time that we live in. It is the time that is told by the clock. It's the five minutes left in time-out. It's being stopped by another red light as you race to preschool to try not to be late *again*. It's holding your breath as you wait to check out at the grocery store while your squirrely boys try

47

48

to rip down candy displays and whine at the top of their lungs about why they *need* M&Ms *now*.

Kairos, however, is God's time. It is time above time. It is a time with no end, when you are able to momentarily stand still in the midst of the hubbub of life and see how things really are. It is stepping back, even in the craziness of life, to take notice of the blessings in life. To realize how God moves, how God provides, and how God simply is.

So, the evening before we leave for the holiday, I decide to head to Chick-fil-A for supper. Get out of the house, keep my kitchen clean, give the kids a chance to blow off some steam in hopes of an extra-early bedtime. Good plan? Great plan.

Except there is a birthday party going on when we reach the restaurant. As if my two little jumping beans aren't enough, let's welcome another eleven four-year-olds full of sugar to a crowded playland.

Serenity now. Tick, tick, *chronos*.

As I sit, watching the chaos swirl in and around me, my thoughts drift back to a moment earlier in the day. Connor had been released from a time-out for dumping out his suitcase *again*. After the time-out, he crawled up on my lap and hugged me tightly around the neck. Laying his head on my shoulder, he whispered in my ear, "Mom, I sorry. I love you all the time. All the time."

And he stayed there, holding tight for at least a minute. *Kairos* took over, and everything completely paused for the moment. Instantly this moment reoriented my life and made me aware of my own haste.

Deep breath. Inhale *kairos*.

Love holds. Love whispers deep and long, cutting through the chaos and reminding me of what really matters in the holiday madness. It is how we love, and who we hold onto.

All the time.

If I forget a toothbrush, it will not be the end of the world. If I don't have the vacuuming done and every stitch of laundry put away before we close up, life will go on.

In an instant, I am reminded by my pint-sized teacher of what really matters. It's not the schedule. It's not the deadline. It's not being overly organized and planning for any unexpected emergency. It is about each other.

Kairos holds tight.

Pausing in *kairos* to embrace the reality of my life with kids enables me to remember what they truly are: blessings, not burdens. And so there, on the sticky, sock-strewn rubber floor echoing with giggles and squeals, I smile.

And take a deep breath of greasy fried chicken air.

Tonight, after I tuck the last of the children in bed *again*, I quietly creep down the hall toward the stairs. Then suddenly: "Mom? *Mom?*" rings out.

Why can't I ever get to the first stair step?

I whip around, trying to temper my complete annoyance at the "one more thing" stall tactic, which just so happens to be the fourth thing of the night. I take a deep breath. Breathing is good. Breathing is very good, especially when you feel like your head is about to explode from sheer exhaustion and utter exasperation. As I exhale, I mutter "God help me" in a less-than-reverent tone. I reenter the room. One. More. Time. If I could only get to that first step.

I seethe out a "Yes?" in my most controlled voice. Then Owen asks, "Mom, will you rock me?"

Generally speaking, I don't have a huge issue with this. But considering the circumstances— that I have already read stories, prayed, sung songs, gotten water, adjusted the night light, fixed the blanket, and rubbed his back—I pause to consider this request. Usually this is when I call in the backup with big letters: D.A.D., who has the patience of a saint. But tonight he is coming off a twenty-four-hour shift at the hospital and running on limited sleep. And tonight is also opening night for football, which he is watching with much anticipation for his fantasy players. (I will never fully understand this.) Considering all of this, I decide to give him the night off.

Just tonight.

But in the silence and darkness I reach out, grunting, to lug this forty-five-pound child close. His legs and arms dangle about as he asks me to sing "Kumbaya."

Now, I don't sing this song very often. Very rarely, in fact. The only time that we ever talk about this sentimental campfire tune is when I retell Owen the story about when he was a wee babe, struggling for sleep.

Do we see a pattern here, Houston?

When Owen was only a few days old, we did everything to calm down our colicky son. Shawn and I would take turns rocking and bouncing, swaddling and shushing, but nothing seemed to quiet our wailing one. Finally, one evening, out of sheer desperation, I started singing "Kumbaya."

Slowly, the writhing stopped, and Owen finally got to sleep. It was miracle. Maybe Dr. Harvey Karp should add this to his five-step baby calming program.

So now, as I hold Owen in the darkness, our shadows stretching and the rocking chair going back and forth, I find it interesting that Owen's one-and-only-song-you-will-get-and-I-am-not-coming-back-for-any-reason-except-for-blood-and-I-really-mean-it-this-time selection is "Kumbaya":

Come by here, Lord.
Someone's tired, Lord, kumbaya.
Someone's cranky, Lord, kumbaya.
Someone's weary, Lord, kumbaya.

I wish I could say that this song works as well as it did when Owen was only a few days old. The wiggling does slow down a bit, and the lamenting and excuses do stop. But those peepers are still bright.

No, the song doesn't work any magic on Owen. What it does is work on *me*.

Like the disciples on the road to Emmaus, I often fail to see that, as a parent, I too am walking a holy path. The disciples didn't realize that the One they longed for was in their midst. But they were intrigued by this stranger who walked with them, talking in such strange, new ways. They yearned to hear more. And so, as their journeys were about to diverge, they invited him to remain with them. How does my own yearning to see God change my perspective and, consequently, change *me*?

As I hold my eldest child—the one who is growing up much too fast, the one whose curious brown eyes melt my heart and whose quick wit can send me into hysterics—and sit there in the stillness of the moment, I sing out from my own soul. I yearn for God to come by and breathe grace upon me. To come by here and to fill and uphold me, even through all the annoyances, exhaustion, and resentment.

As we rock back and forth, I realize that this is all a part of the parenting package. Kids get out of bed. Kids make excuses. Kids need to be sleep-trained. Kids need boundaries. It doesn't happen instantly, however, and it is my opportunity as their parent to teach them with love and grace.

Kumbaya. Because, God, I need it.

He crawls in beside me and lies down very still, his eyes so heavy that I'm not even sure he saw the pillow.

Oh, how I love summer.

Boys run and tumble, explore and investigate, using every fiber of their body and then some. And did I happen to mention that most of this is *outside?* Summer bedtime is so easy. As he peacefully sleeps beside me with my prayers whispered over him, I reflect on the day we have shared. My emotions surprise me. I would expect gratitude, or exhaustion, or contentment. But no.

Regret.

It's regret I feel as I draw my fingers through his tousled hair. I grieve the moments I have lost with my little man. Reflecting back on my day and the day before and the day before that (how far back does it go?), how many times did I push away, decline invitations, redirect, lose my temper?

His love language is time. He desires to be with me, to play with me, to share his little life with me.

"Mom, look at this!"

"*Just a second . . .*"

"Mom, come here!"

"*Wait, baby . . .*"

Yes, we have been in the middle of transition. We have experienced a move that requires packing and unpacking, my husband is still finishing up post-graduate work, and I have writing projects that require time and energy.

It will all end soon, I tell myself. Things will slow down. It won't be like this forever. Then I can engage again.

That's right, I realize, as I gaze into his sweeping eyelashes, heavy with sleep. *It won't be like this forever.* He is soon going to find a new center, have new loves, and enjoy new experiences. Kindergarten will bring exciting newness, and my role as the primary center will begin to be pushed aside.

How am I making the most of these days? Unpacking? Facebook? Email? The heat inside rises. How dare I make these things more important than him? How dare I throw away these precious moments to waste them on things that truly, in the larger scope of life, don't matter one iota?

It's funny: as I unpacked yet another box tonight, I came across a small picture album filled with notecards full of advice from a wedding shower my extended family threw for me. One of the cards in particular caught my eye: *Ten or twenty years down the road,* my aunt had written, *when your life is a whirlwind with children and activities and you can never catch up on your work, make a rule for yourself that you will quit working at a certain time, sit down, relax, and spend time with Shawn and the children. The work will wait, but these moments will never present themselves again.*

It's ironic that I found this while unpacking, which is the very thing that is currently hindering me from being present. *I'm so there, baby. I'm so there.*

I have such a keen sense that time is slipping away. And the only way to truly absorb it, to realize the beauty of the moment, is to be present to the gift that it is. To awaken again to my family, albeit crazy and exhausting at times, to truly engage and enter in, rather than shoving aside and stepping around. Because, in the grand scheme of things, these moments are so, so precious.

Yes, even when boys break yet another light bulb in the lamp by wrestling on the couch. They are little. They are energetic. They love life and they love home and, by God's grace, they still love me.

Do I focus on the light bulb they've shattered on the floor? (What is the count this week? Two? Three?) Do I huff and puff about it and send them off to time-outs again? Or do I focus on the squirrelly munchkins who are begging for my attention and taking it out on each other?

What is it that they really want? That they really need? That *I* really need?

Like the disciples, I have to wonder: *Do I stop and come home? Or do I continue wandering and chasing after answers?* The invitation is set before me.

In the quiet darkness, my heart burns at this question. But I know what I need to do. I need to slow down and engage them—now more than ever in this busy season of life. Slowing down reorients me to what truly fills. Their presence slows me down and invites me to embrace the holy moments all around me, which in turn breathes new life and energy into my soul.

Truly sharing laughter.

Butterfly kisses.

And even gas. (Don't forget that I live in an all-male household. It comes with the territory.)

And so in this moment, I'm embracing the advice from a long-lost card, which is kind of like a mysterious sojourner joining me on this parenting road. Knowing that being present for these little ones (and the big one, too) is just as necessary as the work I do throughout my day, I'm instituting a new Sabbath rule for a new rhythm of life, an everyday Sabbath of embracing and engaging what is truly important: to consciously cease my compulsive need of continual work (*Just a minute . . .*) and to simply enjoy my boys now.

For Sabbath was created for renewal and rest and to remind us that it is ultimately God who creates and holds all things together, not us. Before I blink, autumn will be here and school will start. I'll be sending them off to college, and I'll be swaying with them at the mother-groom dance.

Being present to this one moment, and the next one too, is to give thanks for the grace that has been given in my life.

But a real question nags at my soul. In this fast-paced life in which immaculate homes, mega-themed birthday parties, and bento lunch boxes are expected, the real question might not be, *can* I slow down? The real question might be, am I *willing* to slow down?

Even though I spend most of my days in and around my own home, I often discover that I am not really home at all. I dart to and fro doing things, but I rarely quiet myself enough to settle deep and take up residence with the greater questions of life. How can I welcome Jesus to the interior of my own home, to my internal mess, when I am barely even willing to face up to these questions myself? I busy myself doing things for my family, friends, and perhaps even for God. But maybe this is all just a front to earn approval; maybe I have a need to be needed?

Like Martha in Luke 10, I often feel like I have so much to do, so little time. I feel pushed from behind and pulled from ahead. Is there really any time to just *stop*? Maybe not even stop, but at least to pause? To pause and reflect on why I feel so driven?

What is driving me, underneath it all?

I don't like these questions. And I really don't want to slow down to reflect on them. Why? Perhaps I'm afraid of what I'll discover. Perhaps I'm afraid to admit that I guide my life by the expectations others have of me.

Others' voices too often drive our lives: *Be the best at all costs. Second place is failure. If you don't look good—if you don't have it all together—no one will love and accept you.*

But underneath it all, under all these nagging voices, is the meta-voice from which it all seems to stem. This voice resounds: *You are not good enough as you are. The person you were created to be has fundamental flaws.*

So I continue to over-function in order to gain approval from others and to silence these voices from within. I often believe the lies they tell me about myself. The door to my home, therefore,

58

remains closed and locked. I do not offer a welcome.

Like Martha, we have an arsenal of voices vying for our attention. We have good reasons for believing them. Perhaps someone close to us told us repeatedly that we would never measure up. Or maybe we internalized messages we receive every day, like images of perfect-looking women or men gracing the covers of magazines that lead us to conclude that we are fat, ugly, and imperfect every time we look in the mirror. Or maybe it is the quick assumptions I make when I go to a friend's home and find that it is spotless and manicured, with children that are always cleaned and coiffed, and with a distinct waft of something hot and fresh always coming from the oven. The spit-and-lick technique to wipe the jelly off the cheek and all other attempts to clean up the wrecks we look like are a lost cause when I realize that I am still wearing the yoga pants I slept in and that my son's sock has a hole in it. Fundamentally flawed, I tell you. There are countless reasons why these internal voices scream and yell at us with their varied messages, but what really matters is that they are present, and they have the power to guide our lives.

These voices, these lies, have been around a long time—even way back in the beginning of time, with a woman and a snake. Genesis 3:5 says that the snake told Eve, "Taste this, then you will be like God." In my paraphrase: "You were not created good enough just as you are. You need to be more. You need to be like God. Eat this, for this will then make you perfect."

The bait worked. Eve ate from that tree in the garden.

The lie comes to us still. It might not be from a snake. It might not look like an apple. But these voices tell us to eat more, work more, get more. For, they say, these things will fill our lives and make us complete. These things will make people approve of us; they will take our fragmented lives and make us whole.

And so we take, and we eat.

I find it ironic that in the beginning there was one Voice that spoke the world into existence, saying that created things were good. But as this Voice got to creating humankind, it declared that man and woman were *very* good (Genesis 1:25, 31).

What a spiritual discipline it is, then, to make a conscious choice every day to believe this one Voice—that I am created *very* good, just as I am. Messes and all.

This journey toward wholeness is a continual process that lasts for a lifetime. Yet as we listen to that one Voice calling our name and wanting to enter our home and remain for the night, we begin to hear that we are very good, just as we are. We slowly begin to gather up the scattered, fragmented pieces of life and begin to heal. We, like Martha, slowly come home. We begin to see who we really are. Loved and embraced fully. That no matter whether our house is a wreck or perfectly organized, whether we are overprepared or underprepared, whether we are overweight or underweight, and whether we golf an 81 or

101—nothing can ever change how Jesus values us. For what we do (or don't do) can never change God's love for us.

We are beautiful, *just as we are.*

When we live within this home, we live from a place of wholeness. We can unabashedly open the door, in whatever state our house is in, and become host, because we have encountered the one Host who provides us a true welcome. And from this welcome we are able to welcome (and accept) not only ourselves, but ultimately others, just as they are.

And so I reach for the door and turn the knob.

Welcome home.

EMMAUS ROAD

∙∙

The Emmaus disciples who opened their door and invited this curious sojourner to their home did not fully realize the homecoming that *they* would soon have. For a true homecoming always begins with an open door. Jesus does not push, pry, or go where he is not welcomed.

I have to wonder how this story would have turned out if Jesus—or the disciples, for that matter—had chosen not to stop at Emmaus. The text does not state that this was their home village, although it is assumed. What if, in their own disorientation, they had felt compelled to keep going. To keep pushing ahead?

But it was their very act of pausing, of slowing down, that enabled them to offer a welcome. In time, a surprising gift would awaken them.

How does slowing down enable me to take notice of God coming to meet me? And can I let myself be reoriented to the *kairos* moments of what really matters in life?

Chapter 4

THE OFFERING

....

"He took the bread . . ."
—Luke 24:30

....

I blog. And I enjoy reading other blogs. I recently came across the blog of one of my friends who chronicles her meals in her posts. I was struck at how her suggestion to transform leftovers from meatloaf to shepherd's pie is a lot like my life as a parent. On a daily basis, I am the queen of re-invention. Every day, the challenge is how to get my picky five-year-old to eat and how to dress my three-year-old with a bit more variety. Each day brings new takes on the same challenges.

Yet as a parent, at the end of the day, I often wonder about the leftovers. Because often, after all is said and done, there isn't much left over. If any.

Giving, giving, giving. And then when you think you have given it your all, someone pukes. Or poops. Often all over the floor. But somehow you get up and find the strength to give again. It is a mystery that, where there seems to be none, bounty overflows. Or if not bounty, at the least the need is met and satisfied.

It reminds me of the story about the disciples when they had just come back from an intensive experience of preaching and healing. They were trying to find retreat, space, and a break at the feet of Jesus. But they kept being hounded by more and more people. And more. And more.

The people kept coming. They streamed in from the towns and hillside. And they stayed. And stayed. And stayed. No matter where Jesus and the disciples tried to flee, the crowds followed with even greater intensity.

Then Jesus looked over to the disciples and said, "You feed them" (Matthew 14:16). Feed them all.

The "crowds" of my life hem in. There are little boys, writing assignments, and my marriage to attend to. There are friends and family and the tasks of homekeeping. Haven't these things taken enough already? Feed them more? With *what*?

I, too, feel the rumbling in my belly. There isn't much, if any, to spare.

Jesus' next question resounds to my core. "How much bread do you have?" (Matthew 15:34).[1]

Jesus doesn't ask for a lot. He just asks for what I have. And even at the end of the day, when only crumbs are left in my pocket, I hear, "That is enough."

So maybe this offering is really not so much about how much time, energy, or resources I *have* at any given moment. Maybe, instead, it is more about what I am willing to *share*.

Ironically, isn't this what I am constantly trying to teach my own children to do?

---

1. I am combining two stories here—the feeding of the five thousand, told in Matthew 14, and the feeding of the four thousand, told in Matthew 15.

❧

Like I've said, I've done a lot of jobs in my life. From traditional jobs in education and ministry to the less traditional work of doing commercial voice-overs and weaving baskets: I've done it all.

Yet my vocation as a mother continues to stretch me and shape me and mold me (and some days, squash me) more than any of these jobs ever did.

As others have said, being a mother is the toughest job in the world.

I love my darlings to the moon and back. But if I'm honest, some days I simply am not as present to the guys as I would like. There are calls to make, people to meet with, errands to run. The to-do list continues to grow.

Then finally, when I have a chance to breathe and put up my feet, four big brown eyes greet me. Do I put them off? *Again?* Once again, the question comes: Which part of myself gets priority today,

Mother or *Me*?

Of course the choice is not either/or, but it often feels like it. As a mom, personal time is just hard to come by. I'm not just talking about prayer or Bible reading. I'm talking about more earthy things like taking a shower, sitting with an empty lap, or listening to the news on the radio in the car.

But I'm realizing that as a mother, in order to create *me*, I have to take out *other*: *M(othEr)*.

I know that I am still a woman with gifts and dreams and visions, and I still have a great need for personal hygiene. I do attempt to find balance and space for all these things, so hold your horses before you get all crazy on me. Blessed by many sisters in my life, I spend time with friends. I enjoy going out with Shawn and working on my own personal projects. And I am grateful for the refocus and rejuvenation that they bring to my work at home.

What I'm talking about are those moments, especially at the end of busy days, when all I want to do is crash and my children come near and ask for more. What can I offer?

Mother or *Me*?

I get down on the floor and we play trains, rounding and rounding the tracks. Crash. Derail. Laughter. I have forgotten that sound. It feels and sounds so good.

The blond boy turns and, reaching out his grubby hand, touches my cheek. "Mom, I love playing with you," he says.

Was it worth it? Always.

So today, in this moment, I choose *mother*, because I have found that there are always gifts that surprise and sustain *me*.

As a mother, I find myself in funks every now and then. Sometimes more often than that. Running, running, running: I feel as though I am constantly running, yet I seem to go nowhere. And nothing gets done. Why can't I simply keep up? The clothes are still not put away, the dishes impregnate. And dirt: oh my, the dirt! Where does it all come from?

Two words: *little boys*.

It is just how it is. And how it will be. And maybe, even, how it should be. And yet some days it is just so exhausting. The attitude, the mess, the monotony of this hamster wheel that never seems to stop . . . never seems to stop . . . never seems to stop. Is this the sum total of my existence? To wash, scrub, and feed?

Oh, how I forget.

As I turn the minivan out of the drive to catch a few hours of mama-brain time, here run two pint-sized beauties, waving hog-wild after me.

"Mom! *Mom!* I love you! Happy Mother's Day!" (Thanks, albeit a few weeks late.)

"Merry C'rithmas! Love you!" sings the littlest one, trying to keep up with the holiday cheer.

I smile.

Do I smile because I am going out, alone? Of course, but my heart beams because finally I am able to see. I am finally able to *see*. Getting some space to slow down allows the window of my heart and soul to clarify my vision. *Kairos* awakens.

Boys.

Organized chaos. Of course.

Laundry. Of course.

Dishes. Of course.

Dirt. Of course.

Why do I forget? How can I forget these blessings? They fall fresh upon my spirit, dusting off the tiredness, the monotony. I have been blessed with boys. Messy, crazy, syrupy-sweet boys. I realize that, in remembering these blessings and giving thanks, transformation takes hold. Of everything.

I hope to never forget this life lesson. But I will. As much as I try, I will forget time and time again. And when I do, Christ, remind me that offering oneself often comes before the blessing. Remind me again. And again. And again. Because I'm sometimes hard of hearing.

All I want to do is take a nap. I mean, really, is that too much to ask? Okay, not even a nap: I'd just like to close my eyes and drift off into la-la-land for one or two minutes. But could I do this knowing that my four-year-old is roaming the earth like a free man? Not a chance.

So I'll downgrade my dream from napping to resting to sitting. I just want to sit. For five minutes. Five minutes, *by myself*. In the quiet. Is this really too much to ask?

"Mom, will you play animals with me?"

I hear this question no fewer than one million times in any given week. I am not joking. A million times. Maybe more.

"Mom! Come outside and play animals with me. I want to show you something. Will you, will you?" His eyes twinkle.

I breathe in. I breathe out.

Although a relatively insignificant query, this question looms so large. Why me? Why *now*? *I. Just. Want. A. Nap.*

My needs? His needs?

I weigh the cost of each, knowing that each is valid and necessary.

His brown beauties look at me again with hopeful anticipation: *Will you come?*

Blink, blink.

Will I?

I breathe in. I breathe out. A huge task? Or an honor given?

Day in and day out, the strangers that many of us most frequently encounter are the ones we have birthed. Even though they carry our DNA and have my eyes, Dad's ears, and Grandpa's personality, I am learning that they are still so much their own persons, with gifts to be discovered and realized. And I wonder, *How am I called to meet them, where they are, and extend to them a welcome to come home? How can I meet them just as they are, in all their unique glory?*

"Sure, I'll come out," I say. "What do you want to show me?"

As I walk out the screened porch and step into the backyard, what I see floors me. I have walked into a lush, green savannah. Owen has hidden his animals all over the yard in different "habitats." Tigers in the short prairie grass. Pandas tucked into tree limbs, nibbling on greenery. Pink and green chameleons lurking in the pink and green geranium pot. On and on it goes. As we lurk and creep, Owen tells me of their eating habits and mechanisms for survival. He is one smart dude.

Either that, or he watches way too much TV.

As we walk back to the house together, hand in hand, I realize that what has moved me from stillness to action is that I caught a glimpse of the true invitation. *Kairos* time awakened me to the invitation to meet the Creator—the One whose creative personality breathed life into this budding zoologist in front of me. For this invitation is not merely about role-playing with my son; it is about offering myself to him as he wants to share himself with me. And by interacting and affirming and encouraging those gifts that God has placed within him, I am loving Owen in his own love language—time.

We sit down together on the hot concrete porch steps with blue raspberry popsicles, and syrup drips all around us, making a wonderfully sticky mess of everything.

EMMAUS ROAD

he mystery of enough—the mystery of provi-
sion—comes not in what I have but in what I
offer. It does not matter how much or how little,
because it is Jesus who takes my offering.

In the story of the feeding of the five thousand,
it was Jesus who blessed the offering. It was Jesus
who broke it. It was Jesus who gave those five
small loaves and those two smelly fish and multi-
plied the offering, feeding the crowds.

At the end of the meal, long after the crowds
dispersed, the disciples went out to gather the
scraps. To their amazement, there were twelve
baskets of leftovers. Twelve baskets for twelve
disciples. Twelve disciples who were hungry and
tired, overworked and underpaid. And they ate
until they were satisfied. Coincidence? I don't
think so.

And then in Emmaus, the table fellowship
that opened eyes and hearts through the breaking
of bread first came *in the action of the offering.*
Bread was offered. And Jesus took it. Together
it was shared. The disciples offered to their guest
what they had, perhaps even all they had in their
cupboards, and they were filled in far greater
ways than they could have ever dreamed of or
imagined. They left that table with much more
than full bellies.

Crumbs are all we need.

Even if all I have left in my pockets are minute
morsels, Jesus can transform them into something
that miraculously not only feeds my crowd but

the deepest hungers that gnaw at my own soul. And surprisingly, I find that even at the end of the day, I have more than enough.

Even if I have to restock the blue raspberry popsicles.

Chapter 5

THE BLESSING

. . . .

"He took the bread . . . and blessed it."
—Luke 24:30

. . . .

It was one of those. *Another* one of those days. It had started off so, so well. It really had. I had thought to myself, *Today will be the day I will succeed. I will be more patient. I will be more understanding. I will fill my home with laughter. I will . . . I will . . . I will . . .*

Then came the grocery store. Which could use a name makeover from Giant to Giant Pain in the Derriere. It gets me every time. Every single time.

We all jumped in the car in the morning. Spirits were up and giggles and smiles abounded. I had made sure the kids were well watered, snacked, and potty-ed. We had even spent some time together creating our grocery list: each boy with a marker in hand, scribbling down what was needed. I was ready. I was prepared. I was focused. We made it through our list.

And then came the checkout line.

Of course.

The pause allowed just enough time for my monkeys to climb out of the windows of the car on the front of the grocery cart to reach the forbidden stockpiles lining the aisle. M&M's? Tic-Tacs? Gum? Please, please, *please*?

I think the checkout line is a conspiracy against a mother's last frayed nerve. It is the only plausible explanation. The clerks intentionally go as slowly as possible to keep you in the cattle shoot as long as possible, so that you will be obliged to buy multiple things you didn't think you needed. As you see your children swarming like the seventeen-year locusts, you give in in order not to be completely ransacked. Luckily, that day I had enough reserves of energy to make the boys finally release the hostage items. After a stern look and seething words about expectations and appropriate behavior, they obeyed their mother.

Dragging everyone and our goods in and out of the car, I got us home. Then the toddler refused to nap, the stacks of laundry and dishes grew, the toilet got clogged, and there were constant, nagging requests for snacks every other nanosecond.

I was spent. Completely and thoroughly.

Oh manifesto of joyful parenting, where are you today?

From the highest highs to the lowest lows: that really is the parenting journey. Attitude altitude can change by the day, hour, minute, or second. Snuggling with books to fighting over who gets to sit on my lap. Full-body giggles to full-body wrestles. Bear hugs and sloppy kisses to headlocks and a smear of snot. All of these changes can happen in an amazingly short amount of time. Parenting is a journey of deepest love that embodies both struggle and joy.

Joy is an emotion that subtly persists throughout the ebbs and flows of life. Despite the circumstances, it has the power to transcend and transform my own attitude and perspective. Should I ask for more joy in my life?

At the heart of joy resides gratitude: gratitude for what is. As I look around, I see that I have two healthy boys with kind hearts, smart minds, loving spirits, boundless creativity, self-confidence, a sensational sense of humor, and pure zest for life.

What's not to be thankful for? These dudes are incredible. Busy, yes, but so extraordinary. I have been given so much. Come rain or shine, sickness or health, manners or whines, hunger or fullness, I pray that I radiate joy.

I pray that I will awaken again and see that I already have so much.

The laundry pile is now on the verge of taking over the entire upstairs landing of our house. I climb the stairs to begin what I must do over and over again in this house: ascend a mountain of laundry that sometimes seems to reach above the clouds. As I kneel to the floor, I am struck with the rightness of my posture.

Prayer.

My knees bend low. My arms are folded in lap.

As I reach out to touch the crumpled shirts, socks, pants, and unmentionables, I realize that here I am, in the presence of the Holy.

Worshiping.

I am not in Sunday dress but in workout shorts. My hair is uncombed. But, like I do on Sunday morning, I offer myself up in prayer.

From this posture, I am reoriented to seeing this chore, this never-ending pile, as not a burden but a blessing.

As I bend low, I remember again that this task is really an offering of love, an act of gratitude for my family. My greatest joys and most gracious blessings. Blessings surround and engulf. There are people who wear these clothes (and sometimes change multiple times a day), who wash and dry with these towels, who sleep in these sheets.

Kneeling in the midst of this holy mountain, I, like the Israelites, see the presence of God hovering close. I am like the Israelites who, after the amazing spectacle of the Red Sea, complained and moaned in the desert sun longing for captivity to return.

For these people who were led out in miraculous and astonishing ways forgot. They forgot the One who faithfully led them ahead to the fullness of blessing and promise.

As I bend low, I pray that I not turn my daily duties and tasks, my to-do lists and schedules, into longing for days that are past—for blessings still surround. Blessings continue to surprise and sustain, even in this period of life that can often feel like desert wandering.

Here, at the base of this mountain, I return thanks for the ones I fold for.

And fold,
and fold,
and fold.

❧

Today was one of those days that I hope not to forget. When Shawn does twenty-four-hour shifts at the hospital, I always worry about how the day will go. Yet I can honestly say that today was absolutely perfect.

Sure, there was some bickering. Sure, there were issues with sharing toys, and I needed to redirect from time to time. This is still reality, not some land where unicorns fly through rainbows with leprechauns on their backs. But even in the extreme ordinary that this day brought, it was perfect.

We leisurely spent the day building with Legos, watching Internet videos, and grabbing subs before going to the playground. After baths and books, the boys sleepily crawled into their beds as I prayed and sang and rubbed their backs. At first, they peered over the railings of their bunk beds, their eyes wide open like two little birds peering over the edge of their nest. But in time, each of them slowly fell back on their down pillows, laid their heads down quietly, and drifted off to sleep.

As I sang, I kept thinking, *Stay present. Stay present. I'm in the* kairos. *Remember these moments. Etch this in your heart.*

It was so absolutely normal. It was so absolutely ordinary. There was nothing special or exceptional about it. Yet it was absolutely dripping with the holy. Perhaps it was that Connor called me his "queen" before he snuggled down, telling me how much he loves me with his "whole

78

heart." Or maybe it was so late that they were both just too doggone tired to put up a fight.

Ordinary miracles: here they are.

What makes one ordinary moment feel so spectacular? Why do a million more moments just like it, day in and day out, pass without my noticing them? I think the difference is perspective: my ability to truly take the moment and see it from the inside out. Sometimes I manage to slow myself down and am present in the present and truly able to return thanks for the gifts around me.

Squeaky clean, coconut-smelling boys. Strong boys who are growing up so quickly. Boys who have been given to me to raise and love, teach and shape, nurture and cherish. What an honor. As the songs lulled each one off to sweet dreamland, I gave thanks to the true Queen for bestowing me with these treasures.

"This is what grace looks like," Anne Lamott has written, "amazed gratitude and relief at your plain old gorgeous life."[2]

Perhaps the true miracle in giving thanks is that it completely reorients us to what actually *is*. We breathe: miracle. We have people to care for and be cared by: miracle. We have a home to shelter us, food to feed us, clothes to warm us: miracle.

But how easy it is to forget. How I long for more and more. A sense of scarcity sneaks in and distracts. Yes, I have a cell phone, but an iPhone would *really* make me happy. Sure, I have jeans that fit and look nice, but won't those designer ones be even better? My health report is fine and clear, but what if the doctor missed some disease?

The desire to have more, be more, and accomplish more in my already busy schedule—and perhaps even the compulsion to worry more—leaves me dizzy. I find myself disoriented and unresponsive to the reality of the gifts that abound in my life. It feels like vertigo. Sometimes things just get so out of balance. And it seems the harder I try to rescue myself from the twirling and spinning, the dizzier I feel.

There is always one more thing to attend to. Just one more thing to cross off my already too long to-do list. And I cannot take just *One. More. Thing.* Yet still I create the list, hoping that, once I finally get to the bottom and have everything crossed off, the world will stop twirling.

~~Do laundry~~
~~Finish last night's dishes~~
~~Buy teacher gift~~
~~Exercise~~
~~Review Sunday school materials~~
~~Help Owen with pirate ship~~
~~Clean bathrooms~~
~~Read to Connor~~
~~Pay bills~~

I get to the end of the list. I admire for a moment the scratch marks that leave the paper looking weathered and worn. It is all crossed off.

Yet the vertigo persists.

Why? I guess the list wasn't the answer to re-gaining my balance and controlling the tugs and pulls of this world. Perhaps balance cannot be found with clenched fists. Perhaps taking care of soul space is not an external act. Perhaps trying to fix it externally will never be the solution.

For vertigo is a condition of the *inner* ear.

I look at the list again. What is my soul really screaming out for? Am I listening to what I really need? Or am I merely trying to drown it out because I'm not sure that I'm ready to really listen?

I make a new list. This list is not full of must-dos, should-dos, or ought-to-dos. It is a list from the soul.

Love of a compassionate spouse
Friends who step in and provide space
Unencumbered declarations of love
Cool breeze
Wispy clouds flanked by crisp blue
Sister-friends
Brothers who call
Gift of forming life
Imaginative play
Hockey sticks and active boys
Breath

As I write, gifts of grace are whispered moment by moment in my ear. Is this what my soul is asking me to hear again? These small, ordinary miracles?

That really aren't so small?

With each item on my list, my whirling soul straightens out a bit. Why do I forget? Buying more, doing more, and scheduling more can never entirely calm a soul. But gratitude always restores.

Always.

And so, with my miracle breath, I breathe in grace and exhale gratitude. Maybe this is how we really live. Moment by moment. Taking notice of the miracles and giving thanks for them all.

As our hands circle the dinner table, we sing the overly familiar song every evening, day after day, week after week. Even though I sometimes try to sneak in a new tune, Connor never fully accepts that we have said grace until we have sung "The Song."

God our Father,
God our Mother,
Once again,
Once again,
We thank you for our blessings,
We thank you for our blessings,
Amen,
Amen.

As we sing this song yet again, *kairos* time surprises me. I see that so many blessings surround and that I have all I have ever wanted in life: an adoring and compassionate spouse, children who bring so much joy, family and friends, and a sense of call and purpose.

Blessings truly abound.

Maybe there is something to be said for repetition. *Once again, once again, we thank you, we thank you . . .* For I have a hard heart that forgets. It so easily glosses over the truly good things in life and instead focuses on the annoying song that is sung again, that makes our food cold, and that is accompanied by conflicts over who is squeezing whose hand too hard.

But true reorientation happens as I recall again and again those blessings, both large and small, that breathe over me each and every day. Grace abounds and there is so much to give thanks for. Joy floods over me like a wave. And there is truly only one way to respond to these gifts. The act of giving thanks for the daily blessings of life awakens my dull heart to see the true gifts in my life. To the One who is always present to me, and for the gift of the pint-sized packages that I've been given:

Thank You.

Thank You.

But let's be honest. Some days, finding reason to give thanks can be pretty doggone tough.

Give thanks, my heart whispers.

For what? I want to scream. For cranky kids? For the sippy cup that deposited apple juice all over the couch? For a husband who has yet another twenty-four-hour on-call shift? For my sanity that is all too quickly slipping away? Give thanks?

How? Where? Why? Because *I. Just. Want. To. Scream.*

Give thanks? No. I will not. Dr. Seuss's words in *Green Eggs and Ham* echo in my mind: "I do not like it, Sam-I-Am."

Life feels much too overwhelming at the moment. How does pausing to breathe a word of goodness and blessing mean anything now? (Did I mention that I just want to scream?) The boys' wrestling continues, gaining power and momentum. My warnings and my pleas to cease fall on deaf ears until—yep, you guessed it—it ends in tears. Saw that one coming from a mile away. What to do?

The whispering continues: *Give thanks. Give thanks.*

With every fiber of my being, I exhale through the cacophony of brothers and remember, *tomorrow is a new day*. I surprise myself. Yes, that is a lot to be thankful for. Tomorrow is indeed a new day, a new slate—grace given to begin yet again.

When Owen was born, he was such a difficult baby. Although completely gorgeous and bright-eyed, he gave us a run for our money. Maybe it was just me being a new parent with absolutely no clue what I was doing. Maybe it was colic. Maybe it was hormones.

It was probably a combination of all three.

The only thing that got me through those days was the mantra I repeated time and time again: *I never have to do that day again.* What is behind is behind. I made it through. Hallelujah!

And I realize today, with these chicks under my wing, that as hard as I try, as loving and nurturing as I want to be, I fail as their parent time and time again. Oh, how dearly I love them. But oh, how dearly they wear me out. And oh, oh, how I lose my patience with them. I don't think I have ever apologized more to my boys than I have in the last few weeks. Sleep deprivation and the flu, coupled with the cabin fever of little boys in the midst of winter, do not make a pleasant cocktail.

It can be downright pitiful and ugly.

And so I give thanks for the grace my heart exhales: *I never have to do that day again.* Yes and yes. All is not lost. Thank God for the gift of another chance tomorrow. To be a better mother. To be more patient. To laugh more and upset less. Yes, tomorrow is a new day.

Thanksgiving, although not changing the status of the situation at hand, has the power to radically change the situation of my heart. Offering thanksgiving in this case, although shallowly breathed and utterly forced, still mysteriously empowers me to try it all again tomorrow. Ann Voskamp, blogger and author of *One Thousand Gifts,* writes, "*Eucharisteo* [thanksgiving] always precedes the miracle."[3] What does it mean to pause and give thanks for the big and little things in life that are always there? How does the act of breathing blessings actually change my perspective?

---

3. Ann Voskamp, *One Thousand Gifts: A Dare to Live Fully Right Where You Are* (Grand Rapids, MI: Zondervan, 2010), p. 48.

Sometimes giving thanks is among the most difficult things we must do. While tomorrow might hold promise and hope, it might also hold sadness and death. And when tragedy comes close, thanksgiving can be hard to find.

EMMAUS ROAD

· ·

The disciples sat at the table with the guest-becoming-host, returning blessing for the bread that was offered. My everyday life, too, is a Eucharist meal. Each day, I am invited to bring forth the whole of who I am and the life I have been given—which include losses, both big and small—and to choose how I am going to respond.

As much as I cringe at breathing blessing in the moment of pain or frustration, I see that it is not I who is hosting the table. For this Stranger breaks the bread with me.

Chapter 6

THE BREAKING

....

"He broke it and gave it to them."
—Luke 24:30

....

The sun shone brightly against the crisp blue sky—a true midwinter rarity for northern Indiana. As we headed south on Route 31 toward Indianapolis, the possibilities seemed endless. Shawn was interviewing for a clinical pastoral education fellowship, and his dreams of becoming a chaplain supervisor were close. Our beautiful and healthy four-month-old son, Connor, was sleeping peacefully in his car seat during the sunsoaked ride. Our eldest son, Owen, was not with us; he was staying with family during our trip. I was in the passenger's seat, reading and writing and lost in thought, excited about the possibilities of what lay ahead. Would we move? How might this change our life?

Nearing Carmel, Indiana, Shawn slowed our maroon Toyota Camry to a stop at a red light. We were second in line. Suddenly, from behind us, came sounds of grinding metal and rubber streaking pavement. "Oh, no!" is all that I remember hearing Shawn say.

In the split second that I had to glance in the side-view mirror, I saw a blue car behind us being pushed from behind by a tractor trailer. There was literally no place for our car to go. Upon impact,

Shawn and I were thrust forward. Everything seemed to move in slow motion. I felt my arms and legs fly upward and out, like a rag doll being tossed about. My books splayed open and flew into the windshield, and the taut seatbelt was the only thing that kept me from hitting it too. When I slammed back into my seat, I felt disoriented at first, and then terrified as screams filled the car. They were not my own.

I have to get to Connor, I thought, racing to undo my seatbelt. My fingers fumbled clumsily with the buckle, and as I finally turned to crawl into the backseat, I caught a glimpse of my husband, Shawn.

Blood.

Everywhere.

His nose had hit the steering wheel head-on. "I'm okay; it's just a broken nose," Shawn mumbled to me as I hurdled over the gearshift. "Get Connor."

Thank goodness for car seats. Even though the back bumper of our car had been pushed into the backseat, this basket of foam and plastic had kept our baby free of injuries. For him, the accident had simply felt like a jolt that startled him awake. The car rang with his cries of injustice at this untimely wake-up call, but thank God that they were not cries of pain. Crying, in this case, was a good sign. A very good sign, indeed.

It meant *life.*

Later I would learn that the blue car had bounced off the guardrail, slammed perpendicular into the back of our car, and gone spinning into the intersection ahead of us. The driver of the blue car, a woman, was thrown into the backseat and flung partially out the rear window.

Meanwhile, the tractor trailer had barely skimmed by our car as it barreled ahead and knocked out all the traffic light poles. The cab came unhitched from the trailer and instantly burst into flames. The driver of the truck crawled out of the flames and collapsed a few hundred feet away.

In that moment, as I tugged my screaming baby out of his car seat, I was stunned at how quickly things changed. In a mere second I had moved from a beautiful, sun-streaked morning full of promise and possibilities to one of complete disorientation, disorder, and disarray.

I stood for a moment amid the wreckage, my eyes scarcely able to take in the terror and carnage that surrounded me. *What happened? What is going on?*

Shawn escorted me to wait with our baby in the company of a kindly driver in a white van that had narrowly escaped the wreck. As Shawn shut the door, he asked me to call the hospital to let them know that he would not be able to make it to his interview. Then he carefully walked toward the blue car, stepping through shards of glass and metal, to kneel beside the woman whose body was thrust out the rear window. Her skin was pallid, and he could tell that her internal injuries were dreadfully severe. There he waited with her for the emergency vehicles to arrive on the scene. Once a chaplain, always a chaplain.

As I adjusted Connor, again strapped securely in his car seat, I took a deep breath. It was probably the first real breath I had taken since the collision. I exhaled, and suddenly, without warning, a wave of raw emotion swept through me. I felt a roar of primal, gut-wrenching horror that I can only describe as a tsunami surging through my body. From the depths my tears poured out, and my entire body quaked. I felt like the accident had broken something very deep within me and that my spirit lay somewhere outside of my body, mangled in the wreckage.

I almost died.

Oh my God, I almost died.

I repeated this mantra over and over as the gravity of what had happened took root. *Oh my God, I almost died.*

Looking through my tears at my sweet-faced Connor, I thanked God for one thing: that he would never remember that he had almost lost everything that day.

He had almost lost his mama.

And I had almost lost my sons.

The pain of leaving my children, of dying and orphaning them, was too much for this mama to bear.

The illusion that I had control over my life, that perhaps I could evade death itself, came to a screeching halt. A fear of death, from that day on, was my near-constant companion. It would lurk nearby, laughing at me and tormenting me.

Later that night, as we left the hospital under the shroud of darkness, I thought how fitting the darkness of the night seemed. Although I was relieved to be free from the prodding of doctors and nurses, the X-rays, the CAT scans, and the blood pressure cuffs, there was a darkness growing inside me. Now it was mirrored by this starless sky.

We drove back to where we were staying via the same route we had come down earlier that day. It, too, had changed. After the accident, the four-lane highway had been shut down for more than eight hours. Bent guardrails, missing lights, and skid marks still marked the road.

In the dark, silent car, I mused at how different I felt from the person I had been just hours before. Life, in a moment, had changed. Would it ever feel normal again?

After facing death, can it ever be?

In the weeks following the accident, I tried to convince myself of how fortunate we had been. Accidents like this happen all the time and with far worse outcomes. For us it could have been a *lot* worse. Really. We were *this* close to something far more serious. Yet we walked away with only sore muscles, bruised ribs, a broken nose, and some stained shirts.

What a blessing, right? God must have really been protecting us, watching over us.

We heard these sentiments from loved ones time and time again in the aftermath of the accident. Over and over. We heard them from our family, who quickly came from three hours away to sit in the hospital with us. We heard them from our friends, who were filled with concern and cared for us. Food flooded our table. Cards and phone calls reminded us that we were being remembered.

Yes and *yes*, I nodded. Absolutely. God is good. Praise God. God's angels of protection did surround us. Thank you, Jesus.

And yet nagging questions lingered.

What about the woman who had been driving the blue car? What about the driver of the tractor trailer? *Where was God then?* Did God have a split-second to choose which car to protect? Had we somehow drawn the lucky straw? Why had we been protected and they hadn't? Why couldn't I just be grateful for the life I still had rather than focus on what *could* have been? Why? *Why?*

It just didn't make sense.

This was not the God that I had come to know, love, and serve. I felt that my interior compass, which had always looked to God and felt loved and surrounded by God, was smashed and broken along with our car. I felt as if my life, and everything I had ever known and understood, was now in pieces strewn about all over the floor. Disorientation and darkness swallowed me whole.

Who was this God now?

Two nights after the accident, after we returned to our Goshen home and had begun to reestablish routines and a semblance of normalcy, the night sky grew even darker.

The phone rang. It was not the insurance company. It was Shawn's parents, calling from Florida. Although concerned with our state of affairs, they had news to share of their own.

Liver cancer.

Stage 4.

My mother-in-law.

My breath grew shallow again as we listened to the details concerning next steps. I found that I could scarcely listen. My worst fears were now being played out before my very eyes. I had just narrowly escaped death, which would have left my children orphaned. This was a pain that I could not stand to even think of.

And here I was watching my husband lose *his* mama. Such irony. Such a paradox of unfair proportions.

Questions hounded me. They plagued me. I felt as though I were playing in a theater production of Job. And I was performing all the parts.

I was Job, feeling as though everything was being taken away. My sanity, my comfort, my loved ones.

I was also Eliphaz, Bildad, and Zophar—after hearing of Job's troubles, these three set out to sympathize with and comfort him, but they ended up asking Job to look within and find out what sin was causing his suffering. Likewise, I asked myself, *What did I do?* What hidden sins might I have that caused this destruction and implosion?

I found it difficult to sleep at night. The night, so full of shadows and darkness, seemed to deepen the shadows and darkness within. In those weeks, any pain, sensation, or illness that my body felt spiraled me to a dark place. I felt as though I was constantly running, darting to and fro. I was incapable of being still, because the silence was the most frightening of all.

And oh, how silent was the night.

The rational part of me knew that, having just experienced a bad accident and the cancer diagnosis of a loved one, I was in the midst of a very normal physical and mental response. The recognition that I was experiencing post-traumatic stress released some of the feelings of overwhelming anxiety but by no means completely did away with them.

How could I live life if I was so preoccupied with death?

For this was not living.

It seemed as though death was winning.

I prayed and prayed. *God, where are you in this broken mess?*

One thing I love about summer in Indiana is its amazing storms. In the Midwest, with its expansive sky and flat terrain, one can often see miles upon miles in all directions. This creates a spectacular canvas for these summertime squalls.

As Owen, Connor, and I were gathering up bikes and trikes in the yard after one particularly lovely afternoon of post-nap play, we noticed that the wind had started blowing. And blowing. And blowing. The sky quickly turned from blue to grey to orange-green. We ran for shelter as the thunder rumbled. Lightning flashed. Rain poured. Hail pounded the ground.

Ah, yes: a thunderstorm. And a good one at that.

Safe in the confines of our home, one of our boys opened all of the blinds, oohing and aahing. He was completely fascinated by this natural feat.

The other? Wild-eyed and terrified.

As I held Connor close, his little limbs all twisted around mine, explaining the booms and the cracks and attempting to uncover the mystery of his displaced anxiety, I understood.

For he and I were not too far apart.

I worry and fret and wonder and obsess. From accidents and loss to mud stains and life goals. As I held my wee one wracked with fear, my heart was bursting with compassion for this shaking leaf. He just didn't know better.

I finally got it.

I only see in part. But God sees in full.

I only see the wind, the thunder, the lightning, the hail. The accidents, the grief. In my babe-sense of understanding, some days it truly does seem as though the world is falling apart. The windows of my soul shake and rattle, the ground shifts, and it feels as though life will be like this forever.

But I only see in *part*.

I don't understand how storms work, how fronts come through, how thunder and lightning echo. In my fear and anxiety, I am blinded from seeing the beauty of its majesty and how the rain nourishes the earth.

But God sees the whole.

As my wild eyes look up, I see that I do not need to feel ashamed. For I am held in a loving, compassionate gaze. In tender arms that soothe and caress.

It's all going to be okay.

I only see in part, but God knows the whole. I only see the storm, but God sees the life cycle. And even in the midst of my own displaced fear, echoed in return is only a deep love.

Yes, it's all going to be okay.

Even if I don't understand it all completely, I can trust in the One who does. When the storm dies down, when the extreme conditions of hail and lightning slow and the pounding rain transforms into a drizzle, I can finally begin to make sense of it all. Sometimes it takes a long time for the storm to end or for clarity or meaning to come. In Luke 24, the disciples walked a long way from Jerusalem before the hidden Christ met them. Sometimes, I'm realizing, it takes weeks, months, years, or perhaps even a lifetime. Then, only in the light of the resurrection, do things come into full view.

As the months wore on after the accident and subsequent death of my mother-in-law, I spent a great deal of time and energy processing our losses. As I reflected on my sorrow, I understood that sometimes my vision was so blurred by life that I could hardly see anything in front of me, much less look for the presence of God. And if I'm really honest, I'll admit that in the midst of the grief and pain I didn't even *want* to look for the presence of God. The world seemed just too unfair. At points I wanted to just sprint toward Emmaus, throw up my hands, and give up.

Yet what got me every time when I read Luke 24 was how Jesus sidled up to the disheartened disciples who left for Emmaus. They thought the story was over. How little they knew.

I realized that I don't know the whole story either. I can't see the entirety of how life will turn out. I found myself drawn to the words of Shauna Niequist, who writes in her book *Bittersweet* that "it is sloppy theology to think that all suffering is good for us, or that it's a result of sin. All suffering can be used for good, over time, after mourning and healing, in God's graciousness. But sometimes it's just plain loss, not because you needed to grow, not because life or God or anything is teaching you any kind of lesson. The trick is knowing the difference between the two."[4]

4. Shauna Niequist, *Bittersweet: Thoughts on Change, Grace, and Learning the Hard Way* (Grand Rapids, MI: Zondervan, 2010), p. 234.

EMMAUS ROAD

. . . .

At the table, they gathered together to share in the bread. But the bread that was offered was *broken*.

Much like life. We often feel rubbed raw by life, from things big and small. Yet the miracle of the brokenness is that Jesus is already here.

The disciples gathered around the table with this mysterious sojourner who, through their invitation to enter their home, had now become a friend. At this table, as their fellow traveler received their bread offering, blessed it, broke it, and gave it to them, they finally recognized Who it was.

It was the One they thought they had lost.

With outstretched hands, they understood that, even as they had longed for God, God had been among them—longing for them, reaching out to them, inviting them to *take and eat*. For this was his body, his blood.

Jesus wants to give all of who he is to us. And as he stretches out his hands to feed us, we see the marks of the ugly nails. These hands that hold us and walk with us also know the sting and pain of loss. Truly, we are not alone.

For he was broken too.

Chapter 7

THE AWAKENING

. . . .

"Suddenly, their eyes were opened,
and they recognized him."
—Luke 24:31

. . . .

The sunlight just barely breaks the horizon when my little ones' eyes pop open. This morning I hear the pitter-patter of feet racing to my bed (running, always running). One of my sons gently places his sweet lips close to my ear and whispers, "Mom, Mom! I did it! I woke up!"

Eyes still closed, I pretend not to hear. Maybe, just maybe, he will leave me alone for a few more minutes. *Note to self: buy blackout shades.*

A bit louder he whispers and touches my shoulder gently. "Mom, Mom! I did it! I woke up!"

Maybe if I stay here very still and don't move, I think, *he will get bored and try it out on someone else.* Like his dad. Who is snoozing snug as a bug in a rug next to me. Zonked out, completely unaware of this alarm clock going off. Why do they come to my side, *always* my side of the bed, first?

"Mom, Mom! *I woke up!*"

This little bugger is persistent. I slowly hum and wiggle under the covers, pulling the warmth up under my chin.

Now adamant, shaking my shoulder, he calls out, "Mom, Mom! I did it! I *woke up!*"

As I crack my eyes open ever so slightly, the blurry, distorted image of a big, brown eyeball greets me. *God, please. Why now? For the love of all things holy, let me sleep! It's five o'clock in the morning, for crying out loud! I'm not sure I can do this mothering thing again today.* It just feels like too much.

I never thought it would be like this, with someone always needing something. If it isn't my five-year-old looking for one of his prized animal figurines, or my three-year-old who wants juice now, it's my husband who can't seem to find his left shoe that is literally right there next to him. Someone always wants something from me. Give again? With what? Why did I ever think I could raise a human being? I can barely even get myself out of bed.

In the same moment, I feel guilty for even entertaining these thoughts. For I love these guys to the depths of my soul and back. I would do anything for any of them any time of day or night. I'd saw off my own arm with a nail file if it would save them from harm. What is wrong with me? I am just so bone-tired. Can I do this again today?

Everything within me wants to yell, "Big deal! So what? You woke up! Connor, I am awake now, too—much, *much* earlier than I should be." But by God's grace, I take a breath first. It's these small miracles that I am thankful for.

I sit up slowly, stretching and wiping the sleep from my eyes, and reach out to pick him up and bring him close. Choosing to breathe in gratitude, I whisper back, "Yes you did, Love. You sure did. You sure did."

As we snuggle together, warmth upon warmth, I think about how often I go through life asleep, refusing to completely awaken. Sure, I get out of bed, brush my teeth (most days), and get dressed (if yoga pants that I may or may not have slept in count as getting dressed). I physically awaken. But I often find myself simply going through the motions of life: the making of beds, the loading of the dishwasher, the stirring of the scrambled eggs. I zip up coats, I pat little heads, I drive to the grocery store—all on autopilot.

Even when I am here, I might not really be *all here*. Not in the "I'm losing my marbles" way, but in the emotionally present way. I want to be *all here* in the way that takes in the wonder of the moment, that truly hears and shares in the laughter, that sees beyond the tears and squabbles and the schedule and to-do lists. I want to truly enter into the gift of life.

I look down into the rosy cheeks of my second child, cowlicks of blond sweeping out in all directions like wisps of clouds on a crisp fall day. The fuzz of his footie flannel pajamas are soft to the touch. Where will I be when I finally wake up? Will my boys have receding hairlines and bifocals? Will I long for these days of bare feet and blueberry shampoo and boys who are proud of simply waking up?

How am I being invited to more fully awaken?

One night, back when I was still a minister in Denver, Shawn and I walked in a benefit to raise money for those suffering from lymphoma and leukemia. As the night wore on, we looped around and around Denver's Washington Park. Yet even in the thick of the night, light speckled the sky: all participants in the walk had been given balloons that held tiny light bulbs inside them. These lighted balloons twinkled on and off like fireflies calling out to one another, *I am here.*

As we paced ahead, we approached a group of people who were all wearing matching fluorescent-green T-shirts with "Cynthia's Team" printed on them. It was obvious who Cynthia was. A scarf covered her naked scalp. And here, gathered around her, cocooning and sheltering her, was her team. Holding the firefly balloons, they were illuminating her path ahead. It moved me to tears.

God's presence comes as others hold the light for me when I am unable to hold it myself.

The Light shines in the darkness, but the darkness has not overcome it.[5] There are light-bearers all around me, holding faith for me, until I am able to know it again myself.

Yes and yes. How did I not notice? Truly, God is here. God has not forsaken me, because I can still *see* God at work in those around me in how they offer comfort and care for me, for my family, and for the community and world around them. The love that they exude is palpable. They are bearing the light in the darkness.

Truly, the night shines brightly.

---

5. John 1:5 (author's paraphrase).

❧

Consider yourself lucky for not being a dinner guest in our house tonight.

There are tears. Screams. Flailing. Gnashing of teeth.

Silverware flips off the table as we strap the young one into his booster seat. Like nails on chalkboard, his wails of protest at the injustice of needing to wash his hands before dinner ring out. I'm fairly certain that the neighbors can hear this torture.

As we finally sit around the dinner table, hands extended toward one another literally grasping for grace, we sing our prayer.

"I can't sing!" one of our sons drones. "I can't sing!"

As I hold his little hand in mine, through his sputtering and gasping, I lean over and whisper, "It's okay. You don't have to. We will sing for you."

The weight of these words doesn't quite register as they escape my lips. Only later am I moved by the holiness of the moment. In trying to simply diffuse the situation at hand, I have told my son what I need to hear: *Let others sing for you.*

I can allow the power of God's people to hold faith for me, to sing for me, when life seems to be too much. I can allow them to keep faith for me when it is hard to find, for as long as needed. We need each other on this journey. We are human beings, created to be in relationship with one another. And although this North American culture is full of rugged individualism and resilient independence, we all long for someone to care for, to be loved by, to understand and to be understood.

Yes and yes. God is here. My eyes catch an ever-so-slight glimpse of the everyday sacred. Here in the mess. Especially in the mess.

I smile to myself as I rinse off the remaining green of the pesto sauce from our plates and put the chocolate-streaked bowls in the dishwasher. In the dark, in the hopelessness, in the fear, when God seems to be nowhere in sight, when exhaustion runs so deep, and when even breath seems labored: God comes as I let others sing for me.

I have experienced this singing community, as has my family. Truly, the members of our community have become companions who walk with us. Their love enabled me to begin the healing journey after the car accident and to work through the grief of losing my mother-in-law to cancer. Through their support and presence, I came to see that, even though I might not be able to fully *feel* the presence of God in my own life, I can look around and *see* God at work.

God came to us cloaked as our family members, who dropped everything to come and sit in the ER immediately following the accident and then offered to watch our children to give us space and respite in the subsequent weeks and months. God's arms reached out in the embraces of friends when life felt just too overwhelming. God accompanied us through our sisters and brothers in the church, who showered us with meals and listened silently as I ranted and cried and grieved.

As this community accompanied me on my grief journey, I discovered myself able to sit more quietly and embrace the silence. And it was in the silence that I was finally able to hear the song being sung to my soul. *God is near. God is here. Open your eyes and see.*

You are not alone.

As the night comes to a close with warm baths drawn, cozy pajamas donned, air wafting with the scent of watermelon, I scoop up Connor and sit down heavily in the rocking chair beside his crib. What a day. Per our usual routine, as I sway back and forth in the glider, I peacefully sing for him "his song." Like many parents, I have a special song that I made up for each of my children.

> *Oh Connor, we love you in every way.*
> *Know God loves you too, and walks with you*
> *   always.*
> *May love, joy, and peace surround you every*
> *   day.*

As I rock back and forth, back and forth, the melody lilts to my beautiful towhead, and the sweet words resound to my core.

> *Know God loves you too, and walks with you*
> *   always.*

Connor's eyes close, and he drifts off in peaceful slumber. In an instant I understand, and I marvel at the meaning of it all. For this tune is no child's play, no Mother Goose composition, but a tune straight from the heart of God. In a new way I hear this song that I have been singing all along—before, during, and in the midst of the stormy days following Connor's arrival, including those fateful March days when the swirl of the accident and cancer diagnosis disrupted everything. It is as if I am hearing it again for the first time. The tune? "Be Still and Know That I Am God."

I don't think we can do much to bring on the good in life or avoid the difficult. Life encompasses both fully. It is truly an embrace of the bittersweet. However, God did promise that he would always walk with us. This is most fully seen in Jesus, who came into this world as a sweet babe with the name *Emmanuel*, "God with us."

And so God's invitation in the midst of it all is to *be still and know*. God's invitation to me is to trust that God is ultimately in control. That God holds it all together. It's not up to me. I was never guaranteed an easy journey, but I am guaranteed a faithful companion all along the way.

And here is this song of Connor's, this song that has been with me all along the way. I just didn't hear it. I simply didn't understand the comfort that was available to me the whole way along. I didn't recognize the One who was singing out to me, longing to hold me in the night.

EMMAUS ROAD

The disciples gathered together around the table with their fellow traveler, who took the bread that they offered, blessed it, broke it, and gave it to them. Then, finally, they recognized Who it was.

The disheartened disciples were flush with bewilderment and surprise when they awoke to the stranger's true identity. *Christ? Here? All along the way?*

What was it that enabled them to finally see? Was it the familiarity of these words and actions that they experienced hundreds of times before? The taking, the blessing, the breaking, the offering? The thousands of people who were fed with only two loaves and five fish? The last meal together, when they huddled in the darkness, when he said to do this in remembrance *of me?*

As Jesus stretches out his own hands to feed us, we see the marks of the ugly nails. Just as our own pain and loss can leave behind scars, we know that these hands reaching out toward us know the sting of pain and loss.

For he was broken, too.

It is here at this table—this ordinary place where we gather and offer ourselves, grasp toward one another, and long for God—that we see that God also longs for us.

As we share bread with one another, we open up about our own pain and bleed alongside others. Our eyes open, and we awaken.

For we are in communion with God
and with one another.

Chapter 8

HOLY HEARTBURN

···

"And at that moment he disappeared! They
said to each other, 'Didn't our hearts burn
within us as he talked with us on the road?'"
—Luke 24:31-32

···

Lack of sleep—coupled with two grouchy boys,
freezing rain, and a husband who was on call
yet again—didn't make me the best mama this
morning.

*Rush, rush, rush. Push, shove, move, jostle,
hurry, hurry. For the love of God, will you move?*

As I was about to rage at the world, trying to
maneuver slow munchkins out the door with not
nearly enough caffeine in the veins, the phrase
Life is not an emergency sang to my heart.

I paused in that nanosecond to consider my life
and the immediate need at hand. It was apparent:
right now, no, my life is not an emergency.

Being late to preschool would not make much
of a difference in the grand scheme of life. And
that is the truth. So then I had to be honest. What
is it within that rages? What is it within that
makes me think that emergencies are everywhere?

The laundry pile, the missing shoe, the sticker
on the window, the permanent marker on the
hardwood floors. Annoying? Yes. Emergency?
No.

What is it then? Why do I fret? Why do I worry? Why do I rush and hurry? Why do I forget the bounty of life that is here at the table with me?

Perhaps it is buying into the notion of scarcity—the sense that things are quickly slipping away. That my control is fading. That there will not be enough time, energy, effort, or resources. There is never enough.

But God has given me all that I need. God breaks bread and multiplies the small offering time and time again. For God is a God of abundance, not scarcity. Everything is in God's hands. In *kairos* time I am being invited to notice it, to slow down and see these moments for what they really are.

And they are not emergencies.

So there at the door, with coat in hand, I breathe in again. *Jehovah-jireh*, I breathe. When things really get ramped up in boys, chores, and soul, I say again: *I have been given all I need.*

Bread breaks and multiplies. My eyes are opened, for there is abundance here. Even in the chaos. Such paradox—that where something is broken, Christ is already present. Christ shows up. And Christ is revealed.

I see it now. Strong arms, both big and small, to pull on hats and gloves. Hot coffee in a to-go mug. Sunshine peeking out behind the gray clouds during rush-hour traffic.

Perhaps this is how those two disciples felt as they sat dumbfounded at the table. But it was only the breaking of bread, the mystery shared, that allowed them to see they had all they needed, from the very beginning.

How did they not notice? How did I not notice? I too stand in awe and amazement and with the disciples declare, "Didn't our hearts burn within us as he talked with us on the road?"

April 22, 2011. My own life feels broken apart again. Grief and loss of expectation of life and hope run raw.

It is raining blood.

Again.

Shawn and I have been trying to conceive a third child for six months, with no success. Our previous pregnancies happened very quickly, and we just assumed the same would follow. But January, February, and March have gone by.

No child.

I was so sure that this month would be different. I was so sure that *this* was the month that I would get pregnant. So secure in the knowledge of knowing my body's rhythms and cycles. Yet the disappointment overwhelmed, again. Where did we go wrong?

As I look in the bathroom mirror, wiping the sleep from my eyes, I see the reflection of the disciples of Jesus, who were also so sure that they knew the ending. This time. *This* time would be different. They, too, were sure of it. *This* Messiah would redeem, would liberate, would restore.

And yet, the blood rains.

Disappointment overwhelms. *Where did we go wrong?* they must have wondered.

Jesus, the Christ, hung on that cross alone, wounds gaping. And here I stand, heart torn from the longing for new life that just was not meant to be. My body has failed. Again.

I had assumed that this third round would happen quickly, just like the other two pregnancies. And yet, month after month, no child. Later I would realize that, in the grand scheme of things, a few months are not that long to be trying; many doctors would not even consider it to be a true case of infertility. Later, I would remember that many other families have experienced a much longer road of heartache than we have. Yet, in the moment, the pain of trying to conceive is strong, almost overpowering. A deep longing for a child remains—whether that is after a six-week, six-month, or six-year wait. The deep, gut-wrenching pain of wanting something you can't have—whatever that may be—is so incredibly difficult.

To a certain extent, we all live in Friday.

The world lives in Friday.

And as we live within these Friday nights, no matter what circumstances they entail, they can surely seem long and dark.

One Sunday morning the month before, in March, I had awoken to discover disappointment again. Blood. Again.

"God is in control," I whispered again and again to my aching soul. "God is in control."

As we entered church later that morning, I was asked to read Scripture from 2 Kings during the worship service. It was a passage that I was not extremely familiar with: Elisha and the Shunammite woman. In brief, the woman extends Elisha hospitality, and as an offering of thanksgiving, Elisha declares to the Shunammite, "Next year at this time you will be holding a son in your arms!" (2 Kings 4:16). These words cut to my heart. A son? In my arms? At this time next year? In many ways it felt like an oracle, and yet I knew what these words really meant.

This was a soul reminder: Yes and yes. God was in control and would provide for my needs. And whether or not another child would come forth, I clung to the promise that God holds everything together and would provide what I needed to get through the pain and loss.

Even though my life still felt broken and ripped apart, I knew that I was lovingly held by the One who had known pain and disappointment, too.

Maybe Good Friday—Jesus suffering the totality of darkness and pain, even to the point of death—is the fullest way that he could show us that he has been there, too. That there is nothing that we can go through that he hasn't been through as well. He knows, he has been there, and he is with us. Through it all. We are never alone. *Emmanuel*, God with us, still meets us and stands with us at the table, holding our brokenness.

Agony and pain, darkness and death are not the final word. For Jesus refused to allow Friday to define him. There was Sunday morning. From this I take heart that, no matter how dark the night seems, no matter how desperate our situation becomes, we can trust that there is a Sunday morning . . . somewhere.

Jesus has made a way through the deep, dark Friday night to the promise of a new light found on Sunday morning, and he has promised to walk with us through it. Christ approaches us on the road. Even if, in the midst of the dark night, our eyes are veiled, we do not walk alone.

Life does not end in death.

Christ comes. Just like he promised.

Even as I gazed into the bathroom mirror on that early Sunday morning with crushing sorrow, broken raw with confusion and unfulfilled dreams, I refused to lose hope. For I knew what day it was.

Unlike the disciples, I know the end of the story. Darkness does not win. The Friday night does not last forever. For Sunday is coming. Sunday is there, *somewhere*. And the dawn *will* rise, blazing like the noonday, crushing fear, defeat, and death—even if it's not here yet. Even if the pregnancy test never reads positive again. Even if I make all of the parenting mistakes in the book.

My resurrection sight awakes my inner eye, burning deep to see the life that I have already been given: Owen and Connor.

Such grace. Such grace.

Even in the brokenness of life, I see that I still have so much.

I am still in the hands of Christ.

EMMAUS ROAD

J ust as soon as the disciples recognized who it
was they were sitting with around the table,
candlelight dancing all around, the Christ who
had accompanied them the entire way left them.

It was here at the table that the disguise fell
away and the disciples saw with clear eyes. But
the ultimate paradox? In the very moment in
which they finally grasped the meaning of Christ's
presence, he disappeared from sight. The moment
of greatest recognition was the same moment that
he disappeared *again*.

The disciples must have sat there at their table,
dumbfounded by what had just happened. Eyes
blinking, hearts pounding, heads shaking: what
an incredulous event they had just encountered!
Jesus had appeared to them in the breaking of
bread! And then, he was gone. Disappeared.
Vanished.

But this time, *this* time, joy and hope burst
forth. They had recognized the One who appeared in their midst. The true Host. In the act
of offering and thanksgiving, they were attuned
to receive. They were open to the blessings that
were presented to them, even in their dark night.
And they saw. They finally *saw*. Something deep
within their souls was attracted to this stranger
who had joined them on the road. Their subcon-
scious minds were singing out the entire way to
remain near, to stay connected—for gifts were
present. And so they did. They traveled together,
they invited this guest in for the night, and they

presented him with the greatest honor of hosting the Sabbath table. Their eyes might not have recognized Jesus in their midst, but their souls knew who it was all along the way.

And then in the moment of greatest recognition, when the mind and soul joined, he vanished from their sight. Why? Henri Nouwen writes, "The recognition and disappearance of Jesus are one in the same event. Because the disciples recognized that their Lord Jesus, the Christ, now lives in them . . . that they have become Christ-bearers. Therefore, Jesus no longer sits across the table from the stranger, the guest, the friend with whom they can speak and from whom they can receive good counsel. He has become one of them. . . . Their companion on the journey has become the companion of their souls. They are alive, yet it is no longer them, but Christ living in them."[6]

As we welcome one another, as we listen deeply to those we encounter, and as we extend care to each other, *Emmanuel* shows up. For at the intersection of living and loving, the Spirit of Christ is born.

In this season of caring for small children, it can be difficult to carve out time to intentionally read, study Scripture, and pray. However, as we realize that Christ already resides within us, our lives lived become prayer. For we are working alongside Christ all the way. When we realize this, we stop looking for Christ as something on the

6. Henri J. M. Nouwen, *Bread for the Journey: A Daybook for Wisdom and Faith* (New York: HarperSanFrancisco, 1997), October 5 entry.

outside, someone we need to search for. We begin to see that Christ is already here, encountering us as we go about our daily lives. With the Spirit of Christ within us, we become Christ to the world.

We are Christ's hands and feet to continue his work here on earth, no matter how ordinary, or amazing, or broken our life might seem. As we love and serve others, we do no ordinary task. We play host to our Host, who makes our ordinary extraordinary. We can embrace life and whatever it holds because we journey not alone. For we find our hands, though weathered and worn, are held tightly in the grasp of the One who has his own scars.

Chapter 9

EMBRACING THE HOLY WORK

···

"And within the hour they were on their way
back to Jerusalem. There they found the eleven
disciples and the others who had gathered with
them, who said, 'The Lord has really risen! He
appeared to Peter.'"
—Luke 24:33-34

···

Peter, like these travelers on the road to Emmaus,
didn't know what to do after everything un-
raveled. So he got in his boat and went fishing. It
was what he knew.

Confusion and bewilderment ran rampant.
None of the disciples had direction, and every-
thing felt muddled and perplexing. Seven of them
stood with Peter looking out over the shore of
Galilee, and Peter piped up, "I'm going fishing."
The others piled in behind.

I have to wonder what was going through
Peter's mind as he made his way back into his
boat to fish, again. This was where it all started.
At the Sea of Galilee. On this boat. When he had
first heard his name being called from the shore.

I'm sure just as he stepped into that boat and
felt the rocking of the waves, his emotions swirled
around. *What is happening? What's next? What*

am I—are we—going to do now? Now that everything that we had known is forever changed.

And so he went back to what was known. What was comfortable. What was predictable. And maybe, what was easy. He got in the boat. And went fishing.

As the waves swayed Peter back and forth, I wonder if his heart cried out, *God, where are you? What am I going to do now? I. Don't. Know. Anything!*

It was a long night for Peter and the other disciples. Cast after cast of their nets yielded empty nets. No fish. Another disappointment. The night was so dark. Not of just profession, but of soul.

As the first streams of light were breaking through the night sky, a voice called out from the Galilean shore, "Throw out your net on the right-hand side of the boat, and you'll get some!" (John 21:6).

Reluctantly, they did. But as the disciples pulled these nets back in the boat, they encountered a miracle of tremendous proportion. Their nets were full of fish! And instantly, they knew Who was calling to them from the shore. Clarity shook the night sleep loose.

And Peter jumped into the water and swam to the shore.

As they sat together on the damp sand, Jesus extended his hands toward Peter and offered him a breakfast of bread and fish. After this feast, Jesus turned and three times asked Peter, "Do you love me?"

And three times, Peter answered, "Yes, Lord, you know I love you."

And three times Jesus responded, "Feed my sheep."[7]

Show me.

For love invites action.

For the love of God, get out of the boat and stop fishing.

❧

I hear the voice calling out softly from behind closed doors.

"Mama."

I arise at this sound and go to the one calling my name. I reach down to pick him up from his bed, blanket in tow. As the soft cotton wraps about my neck, I nuzzle him close and whisper, "I love you."

I finally understand.

Jesus asked Peter—the disciple who was lost, disheartened, overwhelmed, and wandering in a crisis of faith and identity—four simple words: *Do. You. Love. Me?*

And each time, Peter responded, "Yes, you know I love you."

And each time, Jesus replied, "Feed my sheep."

Blanket draped across my shoulders, I awaken to what is before me, just as Peter understood what Jesus was calling forth from him. For as I hold this one in my arms and whisper "I love you" in his ear, deep down I know that I am really answering Him.

7. John 21:15-17 (author's paraphrase).

Feed my sheep.

Love requires action.

The care and love and energy that I put into nurturing my boys is ultimately not about me and what I feel or don't feel in any given moment. Ultimately, it is not really even about them. It is the commitment to the path, despite the journey along the way.

It is about the One who created them. The One who shines in their eyes. It is about the One calling out to me that even in the mundane, in the fatigue, in the sometimes tedious work of being a parent: *this is not the end.* Rather, it is the means: the means of loving and serving the Holy One.

Here it is. This is my call. This is my ministry. This is my ordination employed.

Though my primary work these days is parenting, I am still very much doing ministry work.

Quite literally, I'm feeding Jesus' sheep.

Even if that sometimes includes chicken nuggets and chocolate-glazed donuts with sprinkles.

Here, standing before me, is my congregation.

It is a congregation full of dinosaurs and diapers, books and balls. Around my shoulders hangs a stole, of sorts: a fuzzy, light-blue stole with red, brown, and green polka-dots. And I realize it hangs not as an albatross but as an anchor, reminding me again and again of the One who always calls and comes near.

Yes and yes. My gifts to show and spread God's love are still very much in full swing. For

I'm realizing that my mission is wherever I live God's love in relationship. Throughout these years I have come to view my life as being lived to bless others wherever I am, doing whatever. I'm learning that I need to stop striving to anticipate the future or trying to reclaim the past and be more present in the moment—for each is a gift, not to be taken for granted. God has called me today, and that is enough. And I trust that God will continue to lead me tomorrow. I can only be faithful in what lies before me. Being a mama in this short season of life, whether I care for them full time from home or work outside, is truly a holy calling. It is a journey that continually invites me to move toward a deeper awakening of Love. My children teach me so much about the presence of God that comes through the whole of life.

And, although I get tired and cranky some-times, there is no limit to the love I have for these little ones. As I tend to my boys, I live out Jesus' call for my life in the here and now: to nurture and raise them well, so that one day they can come to know and see Jesus and want to follow him.

As I stand holding my little monkey before bed, I remember what is truly important, even amid the exhaustion and fragmentation of this season of life. For here in my arms lies the very sweetness of Jesus in the flesh. I am holding the incarnation, an innocent babe, fresh from God's own heart and entrusted to me and to Shawn for as long as we live.

And as I care for my children, I am reminded that these are the same ones Jesus called near and gathered on his own lap. *This* is the kingdom of God. In caring for them, I care and love the One who created them.

Parenting is holy work. Mostly, it is *work*. And hard work at that. Yet the Spirit warms my heart, reminding me of the important work I am doing to shape lives to bless the world. Although exhausting and stretching, it is so worthwhile, because I am caring for the One who created them. This makes my work both joyful and fruitful.

Here God meets me, surprising me in the midst of my ordinary life, reminding me of what truly is important. Oh, how I need this. Time and time again.

This is exactly why I am ever so grateful for the moments that God breaks into my ordinary and breathes grace over me. For in moments like this, when the Spirit opens my eyes, it instantly reorients, restores, and renews. It reminds me that life is good and that children are such gifts. Yes, they are busy and messy—but it is because they capture the zest of life and explore the world with curiosity.

I pray for God to forgive me, for I am so slow of heart. I pray that God will keep surprising me in these ordinary moments of the holy work I do, so I can get up and put one foot in front of another and do it again. Today. And tomorrow. And the day after that.

So help me God.

EMMAUS ROAD

In the chaos of that moment of Christ's appearing and disappearing, I wonder if the disciples wondered why they didn't see it before. As they paused and invited this stranger within, offered him what they had, and returned thanks for all these things, their eyes were opened. Surely Christ never did abandon them. He was here, and still *is* here all along. Christ is in them. They are in Christ. All the time. The disciples understood how Christ now lived within them and that there was no place they could run where he was not.

How could they stay in Emmaus? How could they remain in the place of running away when all their hopes and dreams, realizations and blessings are uncovered?

No, they could not remain in Emmaus. They had to go back to Jerusalem. They had to return to their spiritual home and tell the others the truth of all that had happened. It was too much to keep to themselves. Their hearts were burning to share this good news.

EPILOGUE

Made Known

"Then the two from Emmaus told their story
of how Jesus had appeared to them as they
were walking along the road, and how they had
recognized him as he was breaking the bread."
—Luke 24:35

One day in April 2012, I stare at the computer screen. I can't believe my eyes.

Blink. Blink.

Me? Write a book?

I stressed out over twenty-page papers in seminary. A book? How? When? *Really?* Do I have what it takes? I am not so sure.

And then, through the terror, I read the line that seals the deal. "I have been reading your blog, *Everything Belongs*, and I like what I see," the editor had written. "I think your voice is one we need to hear, sort of like an Ann Voskamp of *One Thousand Gifts*."

I laugh out loud. Long and hard. I laugh because *One Thousand Gifts* was instrumental in my call to begin a blog about my own journey of parenthood and how God meets me in the midst of it all.

I also laugh because, out of the millions of books the editor could have alluded to at this point, she referenced *the one and only* book that was the precipitating factor in this shift.

Coincidence?

I'm not so sure.

I sit at my kitchen table and reflect on this invitation. I am completely and utterly dumbfounded, and I can't move. My heart is warmed. How have I not seen it all along?

Instantly, it all comes together. The waiting, the pain, and the confusion have all been a part of the bigger picture of Love. All throughout our recent experiences of infertility, I had intuitively felt as though I were going to have twins. Maybe this was because three of my other friends were expecting multiples, or maybe it was just a bad case of Taco Bell. But it was a feeling that I just couldn't shake.

Yet April, May, and June still came and went. Still, no child. And definitely no twins.

Now, as the computer screen flickers in front of me, it all rushes back. *If I were pregnant right now, I would not even entertain the idea of writing a book—ever.* And yet at the core of who I am, I know this request is something much larger than I am.

Everything within me wants to run away. Doubts and fears about my abilities and gifts surface. But just as the disciples knew their home could no longer be found in running away, so too do I know that my own personal invitation has come. It is time to go back. To go back and recount all these things that have happened. To plunge in and take stock of all the miracles that have accompanied me on my journey toward wholeness and call.

I am being invited to be open to God's move-
ment, to say, *Yes!* (or even just a plain, quiet, un-
certain *Yes?*) In the end, these words are not only
mine, but God's words through me. And if it is
not really about me, but God, what do I have to
fear? God will provide all things.

Dare I accept this offer?

Am I willing to be used by God in this way, to
speak to the greater world? With all of my fears
and limitations?

Bread breaks open. My eyes see.

My heart and soul scream, *Yes!*

Because it is not about me. It is about being
open and willing to be used. There it is again: the
act of offering that brings about sight.

And so I reply, "Wow. Yes, let's talk. The
Mystery is at work."

In July, I meet face to face with my editor to
talk details of the book in progress. My deadline?

Nine months. Due in March.

March? Elisha and the Shunammite women
hearken.

A week later, the pregnancy test reads positive.
The doctor confirms the results. One baby, due in
March.

Yes and yes. Twins, for sure.

And I laugh. A journey that began with such
heartache and sorrow now springs forth joy.

Oh, how I laugh.

๛

After four pushes on March 29, 2012, I stretch out my arms and welcome my newest miracle.

With my newborn babe, Zachary Eli, all nine pounds and nine ounces of him swaddled at my side, and a stack of blank thank-you cards piled high, I sit and marvel at the outpouring of grace in my life. Food, clothes, gifts, time, given over and over again. How does one fully name this Love that runs over? As I pour out my gratitude to family and friends for the handmade quilts, adorable baby socks, and unending meals, I find myself writing at the end of each card, "God *is* good." For as I pause in reflection on all these gifts, I am moved deeper into a state of awe. I am not talking about the actual gifts wrapped with paper and string. I am awed by this community of family and friends who surround and support and uphold and encourage. Truly God incarnate is present. Zachary, what a community of love you are welcomed into. What gift.

Looking back, I realize that even throughout the difficulties and sorrow, indeed, the Lord never left our side. God came to us and journeyed through it with us. The name *Zachary* means "the Lord remembers," and certainly God has. And *Eli* is short for *Elisha*, who shared God's promise with the Shunammite woman. I am moved with emotion. Truly, God is good. We are not alone to navigate this world. Jesus, the *Emmanuel*, walks beside us and within us always. Christ accompanies us throughout the whole of life, providing our every need. Yes, there is a lot to give thanks for. Truly everything belongs. Such grace.

Parenthood is a holy calling. No wonder Mary received iconic status. And I have a spunky red-head, a compassionate blond, and a new sweet and juicy bald one to love and cherish, to nurture and teach. They teach me so much about the presence of God that always comes.

I share these stories and pray that my children (and yours) will one day, even in the clamor of this world, hear the continual croon of God's lullaby: the song that tells them that they are loved deeply, cared for fully. It is God's hope, and it is mine, that they will one day discover the fullness of this Love so that they might be transformed in ways far greater than they could ever dream of or imagine.

But I share these stories, too, because often I forget. I forget the blessings that permeate my life and instead am blinded by the work, the monotony, the exhaustion, the pull. Yes, I share these stories as I begin again this mysterious journey of parenthood so that I might be reminded again and again that God never leaves. God never abandons. God always provides. God always blesses—awakening me to see that my ordinary life is really an extraordinary journey full of miraculous surprises.

To the Giver of good gifts, truly, thanks be to God.

EMMAUS ROAD

. . . .

The Catholic Eucharist meal ends with the words *Ite Missa est*: literally, "Go now and tell!"[8] Share this good news, for communion is not the end.

My stories of encountering Christ's presence point to the "*Missa*" that has been given, but I do not have the only story to tell. Others who have encountered Christ's presence along the way have stories we need to hear. These stories of encountering the Holy might look and sound vastly different from mine, but that is the beauty of God's surprising presence. For Christ comes to us where we need it and speaks to us in ways that we each understand.

As we experience Christ, simply being in communion with him is not the end. It is not a special secret to hoard within. It is meant to be shared with others. Find a friend. Reach out. Be real. Because through our own experience of offering, blessing, and breaking, Christ also appears, blessing us all.

---

8. Henri J. M. Nouwen, *With Burning Hearts: A Meditation on the Eucharistic Life* (Maryknoll, NY: Orbis Books, 1994), p. 103.

RESOURCES

A Blessing for Parents

In the same way Jesus hosted the table for the disciples, Jesus also invites you to the table. For it is at this table where Christ feeds us, sustaining us in the important work we do in raising our children. In closing, I want to bless you as well as bless the holy work you are doing.

As you sit at your table, a very familiar place in your home, I invite you to ingest these words as sustenance for your soul. May you be blessed.

May this bread, as Christ's body,
*   empower you.*
May this bread, as Christ's hands, uphold you.
May this bread, as Christ's presence, fill you
*   and give you peace.*
Just as God gave the Israelites their daily pro-
*   vision of manna, just enough for one day,*
may you know deep within that God will pro-
*   vide you with everything you need*
*   to raise your children today.*
And tomorrow.
And the day after that.
May blessings upon blessings surround you,
*   making this task of parenting both joyful*
*   and fruitful.*
Amen.

Questions for Reflection

The following questions are an invitation to deepen your own personal story with Rachel's. They can be used in group study or for individual reflection.

CHAPTER 1: I DON'T KNOW ANYTHING

1. Rachel writes of her bewilderment in early parenthood and of feeling completely unprepared for the task of caring for children. At what points in your own parenting journey have you felt disoriented, disillusioned, or bewildered?
2. When you have felt this way in the past, have you experienced moments of awareness of God's grace and love? If so, how or when did you experience them?

CHAPTER 2: COMPANION ON THE JOURNEY

1. Rachel writes in this chapter about her anxiety about how to merge her profession as a pastor with her vocation as a parent. Have you felt tension between the vocation of parenting and work? How have you experienced that tension?
2. "Love finds. Love always finds," Rachel writes in this chapter. Have there been times in your life that you have felt God's love finding you?
3. "Maybe opening my arms wider to embrace the reality of what my life is full of now, rather than crossing my arms tighter and refusing to give any more, is how to get through these crazy days and find fulfillment," Rachel writes. Do you agree?

CHAPTER 3: SLOWING DOWN, COMING HOME
. . . .

1. "[T]he only way to truly absorb it [the passage of time], to realize the beauty of the moment, is to be present to the gift that it is," Rachel writes. How do you experience the passage of time as you parent your children? Are there days or weeks or months that seem to go faster or slower than others?

2. Rachel also writes about instituting a Sabbath rule: "an everyday Sabbath of embracing and engaging what is truly important." What practices or habits help you to experience Sabbath moments in your day or week?

3. Rachel confesses that she often catches herself being driven by others' expectations of her. In what ways do you find that you respond less to God's call in your life than to other people's needs or expectations?

4. What messages do you receive from society, family, friends, or church about what kind of person you should be? What do you do in response to those messages? Can some of those messages be redeemed, or are they mostly negative?

CHAPTER 4: THE OFFERING

. . . .

1. Using the story of when Jesus fed the five thousand, Rachel suggests that it often feels like the "crowds" of her life also hem her in, needing something from her. Who make up the "crowds" in your life?

2. What do you think Rachel means when she says, "Maybe it is not so much about how much time, energy, or resources I *have* at any given moment. Maybe, instead, it is more about what I am willing to *share*"?

3. Have you ever thought that you had no more energy or time left to give and then discovered otherwise?

4. Are there dangers of giving too much of yourself away to children, church, work, or friends? How do you discern how much of your time and energy to give to others?

CHAPTER 5: THE BLESSING

1. Rachel talks about how the desire to "have more, be more, and accomplish more" and even "worry more" leaves her disoriented and weary. Do you identify with these desires for more? If so, have you learned strategies or practices that help you manage them?

2. Reflect on this statement: "Thanksgiving, although not changing the status of the situation at hand, has the power to radically change the situation of my heart." When have you felt your heart altered by thanksgiving?

3. Have you ever made lists of things that you are grateful for? What effect has such a practice had on you?

4. Has your family found ways to make thanksgiving a part of your life together? What practices of gratitude have you found meaningful?

CHAPTER 6: THE BREAKING

1. A car accident and a cancer diagnosis of a loved one brought Rachel to what felt like a breaking point. What experiences in your life have been breaking points for you?

2. The accident and cancer diagnosis made Rachel question the character of God and the seeming randomness with which tragedy strikes. Have you struggled with the question of God's providence in the midst of tragedy? What comforts or consolations have you found in such times?

CHAPTER 7: THE AWAKENING

1. Rachel writes about a time when she could have scolded her son for waking her up early. "But by God's grace, I take a breath first," she writes. "It's these small miracles that I am thankful for." What small miracles of parenting have you experienced?

2. "I can allow the power of God's people to hold faith for me, to sing for me, when life seems to be too much," Rachel says in this chapter. "I can allow them to keep faith for me when it is hard to find, for as long as needed." When have you allowed your church community to carry your faith for you?

CHAPTER 8: HOLY HEARTBURN

1. What do you think Rachel means when she writes, "Such paradox—that where something is broken, Christ is already present"? Have you experienced this paradox in your own life?

2. "We are Christ's hands and feet to continue his work here on earth, no matter how ordinary, or amazing, or broken our life might seem." When do you most clearly experience this sense of being Christ's hands and feet in the world?

CHAPTER 9: EMBRACING THE HOLY WORK
. . . .

1. Rachel compares Christ's call to Peter to "feed my sheep" with her call as a parent. Do you agree that caring for children is a way to live out Christ's call to feed his sheep? How do you experience that call in your life?

2. In what ways is parenting similar to pastoral ministry?

3. Do you think most churches affirm a call to parenting? What might the church do to bless and nurture parents, especially parents of young children?

4. What blessings might you offer to younger people who are beginning this journey of parenting?

ACKNOWLEDGMENTS

Writing a book with three small children at home is a testament to the community that surrounded and sustained me, waiting for this "baby" to come forth. This book could never have happened without the faithful companions who walked with me through this process.

My deepest thanks go to those who faithfully loved on, cared for, and supervised my boys, making space for me to write. Kristin Sancken was not only a wonderful help with my boys but also offered hours of reading really bad drafts, and was above all a really good friend. Marilyn Koleczar provided way more than babysitting services; she was the modern-day Mary Poppins. And my mother, Barb Springer, tirelessly went above and beyond the call of grandparent duty to not only care for the boys for weeks at a time when deadlines closed in but also kept my immediate family afloat. She fed us delicious meals, tamed the laundry, washed my windows, stocked my freezer, helped with homework, and ironed shirts that would have otherwise been put into the "de-wrinkle" cycle again. Her dedication to family, deep faith, and constant support have taught me how to love my own family well, and I hope that one day my own boys will think as highly of me as I do of her.

Thanks to my editor Byron Rempel-Burkholder, who encouraged me to listen deeply to the voice that resided within. And to my other editor

142

Valerie Weaver-Zercher, whose timely feedback and brilliant suggestions for structure and flow has made me realize that the real writers in this world are editors. I am eternally grateful. And, of course, to the editor in chief of Herald Press, Amy Gingerich, who caught a vision for this book in the first place and invited me to consider this project. Thank you.

Much gratitude is due to Rachel Whitmer, Sarah Miracle, and Heidi Miller, who generously read drafts and offered thoughts and suggestions at various points of the manuscript. Their encouragement for me and for what God was calling forth from me was invaluable.

For the prayer and moral support of those from Charlottesville Mennonite Church, I am thankful beyond words. Thank you for also providing the space for me to write. And thanks to Roy and Maren Hange, my pastors and my friends as well, for deep listening and wise counsel.

I am blessed to be surrounded by such amazing friends who never told me to my face just how tired they were of me talking about "the book." Their genuine interest and cheer gave me such joy. I am especially grateful for friends Meredith Curs, Jen Skipper, Charlie Palumbo, Jen Shenk, Mandy Yoder, Becca Shank, Carrie Martens, Chet and Mary Denlinger, Tim Sams, Elizabeth Killian, Ivonne Lopez, Anna Brown, Sara deGoa, Joanna Miller, Ann Schrock, Ashley Blurton, and all the wonderful ladies and mentor moms at Charlottesville MOPS. You championed me to continue to seek God and find joy and meaning in the sometimes crazy life at home—it is all worth it (3 John 1:4).

I am grateful for the boundless support of my family, who, if all else fails, I know that I can count on to buy at least one copy of this book. Much gratitude is due to my brothers, Ross Springer, Troy Springer, and Tyler Springer—because they have truly prepared me for raising boys. Life wouldn't have been the same if we didn't have "all three." And to my dear sisters-in-law, Amy Springer, Catie Froese Springer, and Sara Springer, who have taught me so much about creating a home. To my father, Roger Springer, who taught me the spirit of generosity and holding life loosely. His deep support for me, no matter what crazy project I'm up to, means the world. And to Keith Gerber and Kent and Miriam Gerber, who have been vigorous in finding resources and have had a steadfast belief in this book: a sea of thanks a million times over.

This book would have never even been conceived if there had not been so many loyal readers of my blog, *Everything Belongs* (www.everything-belongs.com). Thank you for showing up and reading my very inconsistent posts; more importantly, thank you for allowing the Spirit of God to work through me in this forum. And thanks to my ultimate webmaster, Tim Blaum, whose gift to the media world is outstanding.

And to my boys, Owen, Connor, and Zachary: without you there would be no blog and no book. I love you to the moon and back infinity times over. Your creativity, humor, boundless energy, and love have taught me so much about how God surprises me in the midst of life. It is an honor to be your mother; if I could do it all again, I would in a heartbeat. Sleep deprivation, stretch marks, and all.

And finally, I want to thank my amazing husband, Shawn Gerber. Shawn is my best friend, closest confidant, most dedicated coparent, and love of my life. In many ways he made this book possible, often putting aside his own agenda. Shawn, you have always been my biggest fan, and have encouraged me to do things that I thought were far beyond me. Because of your unwavering support for this book, it is in many ways as much yours as it is mine. I am so thankful to have a true partner like you, and I can think of no one else I would rather traverse these years with.

THE AUTHOR

Rachel S. Gerber, of Bloomington, Indiana, is an ordained minister in the Mennonite Church USA and the proud mama of three boys. With degrees from Eastern Mennonite Seminary and Goshen College and experience pastoring Mennonite congregations in Colorado and Indiana, she currently serves part time as the Mennonite Church USA denominational minister of youth and young adults. She also writes for a variety of publications—all the while working simultaneously with diapers, dishes, and dinosaurs. Rachel enjoys speaking, traveling, and a cup of good, dark-roast coffee.